Information Systems Engineering Library

Managing Reuse

April 1994

London: HMSO

The Government Centre for Information Systems

Information Systems Engineering Library
Managing Reuse

© **Crown Copyright 1994**

Applications for reproduction should be made to HMSO

First published 1994

ISBN 0 11 330616 4

For further information regarding this volume and other CCTA products please contact:-

CCTA Library,
Riverwalk House
157-161 Millbank
LONDON
SW7P 4RT

071 217 3331

Foreword

The Information Systems Engineering Library provides guidance on managing and carrying out Information Systems Engineering activities. In the IS life-cycle, Information Systems Engineering takes place once the IS strategy has been defined. It is concerned with the development and ongoing improvement of information systems up to the operational stage, and their maintenance whilst in operational use.

The Information Systems Engineering Library builds on guidance in the CCTA IS Guides, particularly set A: Management and Planning Set and set B: Systems Development Set and complements other CCTA products, in particular the project management method, PRINCE, and the systems analysis and design method, SSADM.

Volumes in the Information Systems Engineering Library are of interest to varying levels of staff from IS directors to IS providers, helping them to improve the quality and productivity of their IS development work. Some volumes in this library should also be of interest to business managers, IS users and those involved in market testing, whose business operations depend on having effective IS support by means of Information Systems Engineering activities.

The Information Systems Engineering Library also complements other related CCTA publications particularly the Programme and Project Management Library, the Information Management Library for data management issues, the IT Infrastructure Library for operational issues and the IS Planning Subject Guides for strategic issues.

CCTA welcomes customer views on Information Systems Engineering Library publications. Please send your comments to:

Information Systems Engineering Group
Gildengate House
Upper Green Lane
NORWICH
NR3 IDW

Acknowledgements

The assistance of David Whitgift of Logica, David Gradwell of Data Dictionary Systems Ltd, John Hall of Model Systems and Brent Work and David Bowers of Surrey University is gratefully acknowledged.

Contents

Chapter			page
		Foreword	3
		Acknowledgements	4
		Contents	5
1		**Introduction**	7
	1.1	Purpose	7
	1.2	Who should read this volume	8
	1.3	Assumed knowledge	8
	1.4	Structure of this volume	8
2		**Overview**	11
	2.1	Aspects of reuse	11
	2.2	Key messages	11
3		**What is reuse?**	13
	3.1	By definition and by analogy	13
	3.2	Kinds of reuse	14
	3.3	Levels of reuse	15
	3.4	Examples of reuse	16
	3.5	Reuse throughout the information system life-cycle	18
	3.6	Exploiting a reusable component to change a business	19
	3.7	Sources of reusable components	19
4		**Benefits, costs and risks**	21
	4.1	The benefits	22
	4.2	The costs	23
	4.3	The risks	25
5		**Reuse in application development**	27
	5.1	What do users want from information systems?	27
	5.2	A conceptual schema for information support	29
	5.3	A 3-schema specification architecture	31
	5.4	Reuse in the 3-schema specification architecture	36
	5.5	Types of reuse within SSADM	38
	5.6	What is an SSADM reusable component	40
	5.7	Tailoring SSADM for reuse	42

6		**Enabling methods and technologies**	43
	6.1	Design methods	43
	6.2	Reverse engineering	46
	6.3	Repository technology	48
	6.4	Open systems	52
7		**Planning for reuse**	57
	7.1	Key messages	57
	7.2	Getting started	57
	7.3	Who decides	59
	7.4	Deciding whether to reuse	60
	7.5	Managing risk	63
	7.6	The need to change the culture	65
	7.7	Management support	65
	7.8	Organisational capability	65
	7.9	The Project Initiation Document	66
	7.10	Providing personal incentives	66
	7.11	Training for Reuse	67
	7.12	When software development is contracted out	68
	7.13	Measuring reuse	68
8		**Building and managing component libraries**	69
	8.1	Managing the library of reusable components	69
	8.2	Searching for reusable components	71
	8.3	Adding a new component to the library	72
	8.4	Configuration management	72
	8.5	When to invest in new reusable components	75
	8.6	Functional attributes	77
	8.7	Quality attributes	78
9		**Inter-project roles and responsibilities**	81
	9.1	Management direction and technical work	81
	9.2	Inter-Project Boards	81
	9.3	The Component Management Team	82
	9.4	Organisational relationships	84
	9.5	Examples of organisational structures to support reuse	86
A		**Tailoring SSADM for reuse**	89
	A.1	Tailoring SSADM techniques	89
	A.2	Tailoring activities and information flows	90
B		**Bibliography**	109
C		**Glossary**	111
		Index	117

1 Introduction

1.1 Purpose

The purpose of this volume is to provide guidance on the management of reuse to those responsible for exploiting reuse on IS development projects.

The volume aims to describe:

- what reuse is

- the benefits, costs and implications of reuse for projects developing or maintaining IT systems

- the management techniques which are most effective in promoting reuse alongside current CCTA guidance, such as the methods PRINCE and SSADM, and in association with current technology.

Reuse in information systems engineering is the adoption of an existing component of an information system as opposed to designing or developing a new component for that specific project. Components can also be designed from the outset to be reused. Reusable components can cover the system life-cycle from requirements to code and include processing as well as data. Components range from business models through design components to common elements of code. Components can originate from outside the adopting project, for example, from another project or from a third party supplier.

Three kinds of reuse are considered:

- 'tailoring' reuse: modifying a copy of an existing component

- 'copy' reuse: using a copy of an existing component without changing it

- 'true' reuse: using an existing implemented component (not a copy of it).

Reuse of code within projects is relatively well known and understood.

This volume takes both a single project view and an inter-project view of information system development and maintenance which emphasises the importance of co-ordination between individual projects.

The likely benefits and pitfalls of the different kinds of reuse are discussed, together with the management issues which need to be addressed when reuse or wider reuse of components is being planned.

1.2 Who should read this volume

This volume should be read by:

- managers responsible for programmes or projects involving information system development and maintenance and associated project personnel, including managers of project support offices

- those responsible for defining and implementing IS policies concerned with system development

- heads of the data management function and their staff

- managers responsible as 'intelligent customers' for specifying, obtaining and overseeing IS development and maintenance services.

1.3 Assumed knowledge

Readers are assumed to be familiar with the basic concepts of information systems development. Some readers may need to refer to publications listed in the bibliography (Annex B).

1.4 Structure of this volume

Chapter 2 gives an overview of this volume.

Chapter 3 defines and illustrates reuse.

Chapter 4 describes the benefits, costs and risks of reusing components.

Chapter 5 discusses reuse in the context of application development including SSADM-based application development.

Chapter 6 addresses enabling methods and technologies.

Chapter 7 covers planning for reuse.

Chapter 8 describes the management of the organisation's library of reusable components and gives guidance on the production of new reusable components.

Chapter 9 looks at the inter project role and responsibilities

Annex A gives an example of tailoring SSADM for reuse.

Information Systems Engineering Library
Managing Reuse

2 Overview

2.1 Aspects of reuse

Reuse is an approach to information system (IS) development which, if properly managed, can be more economical and produce better quality systems than conventional approaches. This volume offers guidance on the subject and:

- explains the types of reuse, stressing their relevance to all stages of the IS project life-cycle

- describes the costs, benefits and risks of reuse

- describes when a project should reuse a component and when it should develop a new reusable component

- summarises the technologies needed to make reuse feasible

- characterises what makes a good reusable component, so that project managers knows what to look for and when and how to build them

- describes the opportunities for reuse at various stages of the information system life-cycle

- outlines the organisational structure needed to make reuse happen

- summarises two roles (the Inter-Project Board and the Component Management Team) which are needed for effective reuse between projects.

Reuse will not happen without components to reuse. Individual projects will not produce reusable components without direction or incentives. Inter-project roles are needed to co-ordinate reuse between projects.

2.2 Key messages

This volume delivers the following messages:

- We might get more for our money: there are benefits in reusing existing components rather than developing new ones - cost, development time, testing, robustness

- Nothing comes free: there are overheads in specifying, designing and building reusable components, and keeping them in accessible libraries

- Reusability can happen by intent or by accident: we should plan for intended reuse and regard accidental reusability as a bonus

- Sometimes we get it wrong: the overheads of creating and maintaining some components that we hoped would be reusable turn out to be not worth the benefit we get from them. This should not make us give up, but we have to manage the trade-off

- Reuse can happen at several levels: requirements, specifications, designs, code. Almost all the real experience is in two areas:

    - code

    - copying of data specifications from corporate data models.

3 What is reuse?

3.1 By definition and by analogy

Reuse may be defined as the adoption of an already created component in preference to the design and construction of a new component. Components can be designed from first principles to be reusable.

Reuse is much more widespread in other engineering disciplines than it is in IS development. The designer of a chemical plant wherever possible assembles a design from existing off-the-shelf components such as heat exchangers and distillation columns. A computer hardware designer would not design new chips for a new personal computer but, using his knowledge of component catalogues, would use existing integrated circuit components.

IS application systems have up to now been built in craftsmen mode ie built from scratch to meet specific user requirements rather than by assembling a system from existing available components. With the growth of object-oriented (OO) and other techniques the likelihood of commercially available off the shelf components becomes greater. Application development teams have the opportunity to make available reusable components at the organisation level.

The objective of this volume is to encourage reuse in IS application development. However, it must be recognised that the components of an information system are usually more complex than those in other engineering disciplines, so finding and reusing an existing component is more difficult. Furthermore, reuse in information systems may involve modifying a component before it can be reused. Additionally this volume seeks to encourage IS developers to consider designing components for reuse.

The costs, risks and benefits of reuse are discussed later in this chapter but, in principle, it should be cheaper to reuse a component than to redesign it. Maintenance costs should be reduced and the quality of the information system should be improved. When a component is designed explicitly for reuse then the potential savings are even greater.

3.2 Kinds of reuse

We can classify different kinds of reuse. The first we could call *tailoring reuse*: this means adapting a copy of an existing component to make a new one. This is indirect reuse. It is more widespread than *direct reuse*, but less effective.

One hope is that tailoring reuse will be well supported in object-oriented environments (see Chapter 6), by creation of new subclasses with inheritance and (perhaps) cancellation. However, this technology is immature for objects with persistent data (which are mostly what the guide is concerned with). Areas where further experience is needed include:

- mechanisms for implementing inheritance with persistent data

- restructuring of the logical data model (LDM) around the superclass after implementation of subclasses.

Direct reuse means using a component without changing it. The component is used without any development or internal testing effort - only the interfaces between it and other components have to be tested. There are two kinds of direct reuse:

- Copy reuse (sometimes called *cloning*): making a copy of an existing component to use in a new environment or system

- True reuse: extending the use of an existing component. It may involve using existing object instances, or creating new instances of existing object classes.

True reuse is possible only within the scope of one system, or where a shared server exists as an external system.

An IS development project can reuse a wide variety of IS components including:

- fragments of code, such as subroutines

- larger components of code, for example, a database management system
- the results of the analysis of a business area
- the results of the design of a part of a system
- test data
- business procedures
- development tools
- data specifications from a corporate data model.

3.3 Levels of reuse

This section gives several examples of component reuse. The objective is to highlight to the reader the wide range of opportunities for reuse during the development of an IS. The examples below are presented in approximately the order in which the reuse occurs in the information system life-cycle.

The extent of reuse within an organisation may be classified as being at one of the following levels:

- *Level 1: Ad hoc Reuse.* Reuse is not managed and is not easily repeatable. Reuse occurs when individual programmers reuse their own subroutines or, if they happen to know about them, other programmers' sub routines

- *Level 2: Project Reuse.* Reuse is a by-product of the development process and is encouraged by the Project Board. It typically involves reuse of off the shelf components and reuse between members of the same project team

- *Level 3: Institutionalised Reuse.* Reuse is an explicit part of the development process and occurs between, as well as within, projects. It is promoted by organisational structures such as those described in Chapter 9 of this volume

- *Level 4: Broad Spectrum Reuse.* Reuse is part of the corporate culture and is central to the development process. There are incentives for reusing components and for producing new reusable components. Systems are assembled by combining together reusable components.

There is level 1 reuse within all organisations and level 2 reuse within many. An objective of this volume is to help increase reuse within government organisations to level 3 and, ultimately, to level 4.

3.4 Examples of reuse

Reuse of business analysis

The Ordnance Survey has developed a data model for spatial data as part of the work on its Topographic Data Management System. This is a generic model of spatial data which can be specialised for specific applications. This is leading to savings in analysis time for new Ordnance Survey spatial data projects. Ordnance Survey is seeking industry agreement for the spatial data model and if this is achieved, it will make the systems analysis task easier for a wide range of Ordnance Survey's customers.

In the National Health Service (NHS), the Information Management Centre has developed a generic business model of the NHS, called the Common Basic Specification. This is being used by many hospitals to help them to procure application software.

Business templates

There is now a supply of business templates which cover areas such as purchase ledgers and payroll systems. Developers build on these templates to develop applications tailored to their particular requirements. For example a UK business equipment leasing firm has purchased one of these templates and claims that it can build bespoke properly-integrated systems within a reasonable cost and timescale. Before adopting this technology, the firm would have had to buy a number of packages which would then need to be integrated.

Organisations can build and exploit their own templates. A complex frequent flyer system was

> Chapter 3
> What is reuse?

developed by the US airline TWA using the JMA technology. TWA then sold this system to Canadian Airlines which claims to have tailored the system with little effort.

Reusable components at the Inland Revenue	The Inland Revenue is rewriting its Corporation Tax Pay and File system. This major programme is organised as a series of seven projects each of which produces Logical Units of Manageable Proportions (LUMPs) and Corporate Logical Units of Manageable Proportions (CLUMPs) as well as reusing CLUMPs from other projects in the programme. CLUMPs extend the reuse of business analysis components to design and implementation. A CLUMP is a component which is reused between projects in the programme. A CLUMP typically corresponds to a subject area in the data model for the system, for example, there is a CLUMP for the taxpayer entity and closely related entities. Reuse between projects is coordinated by an architecture team which maintains a broad but essentially shallow view of each project throughout its life-cycle. The architecture team uses object-oriented methods to model CLUMPs so that, for example, the taxpayer CLUMP has associated operations which characterise its behaviour. Each of the individual projects uses SSADM.
An off the shelf package	Off the shelf packages range from word processing and spreadsheet products to complete manufacturing packages, such as ICL's OMAC or IBM's COPICS. The accounting package mentioned in section 3.6 is another example of such a package.
An application kernel	The utilities group of a software house develop Supervisory Control and Data Acquisition (SCADA) systems for many clients that are independent of each other, for example, gas, water and electricity companies. Each system is usually developed from kernel software which provides the basic functions common to all SCADA systems. A SCADA system for

a particular client builds upon this kernel to meet the client's specific requirements.

The decision to reuse the SCADA kernel is usually made when the software house tenders for the development of a system. The ultimate basis for this decision is whether reusing the SCADA kernel allows the company to bid a lower price for the development.

System software

The designer of a payroll application must provide facilities for storing data on disc and for the input and output of data. The most cost effective way of providing these facilities is to use a database management system, for example Oracle, Ingres or DB2, and a user interface system, for example Motif or Microsoft Windows.

Systems of these sorts, often called basic software or middleware, allow the designer to concentrate on the core business aspects of the payroll application. Designers of applications should not attempt to re-invent middleware.

3.5 Reuse throughout the information system life-cycle

Traditionally the components which have been most successfully reused are the first and second types of component in the list in 3.3. It is important, to note, however, that there are opportunities for component reuse throughout the IS life-cycle. Every stage of a project may reuse components from a library and provide reusable components to a library.

The benefits of reuse are greater earlier in the life-cycle for the following reasons:

- once the decision is made to reuse a design then it is possible that the implementation of that design will also be reusable. This implementation reuse requires traceability from the design to its implementation. Sometimes a design for which there is no implementation as code may be reused, but this is the exception rather than the rule

- the reuse of a component of code often requires that the system is designed around the component. For example, the decision to reuse an existing set of routines to calculate personal taxation in a tax collection system influences the specification and design of the system and may influence its feasibility. If reuse is not considered until the design stage of the project, then reusing a component may require substantial rework of previous stages.

3.6 Exploiting a reusable component to change a business

The usual approach to reuse is to identify components that fit within the existing organisational framework. It is however sometimes appropriate to consider a more radical approach and adopt a large scale reusable component which changes current business practice.

To give an example, a government department became aware of the need to relate revenue earned from its consultancy business to the costs incurred in providing it. As the department had little experience of commercial accounting practice having been cash-based up to that point, it felt that there was little point in expending research on analysing the requirements in detail and had little knowledge of alternative business methods. It made more sense to purchase a complete reusable component that included business procedures, accounting standards and supporting computer software.

3.7 Sources of reusable components

There are supply and demand sides to reuse. A component must be produced before it can be reused. A component may be produced by another project within the same organisation, or by another organisation.

Normally, the organisation responsible for producing a reusable component is responsible for its integrity. If the reusable component comes from a third party supplier, then the project normally relies on that third party to maintain the component, although this reliance itself constitutes a risk which must be assessed and managed.

If the reusable component originates from within the organisation then the organisation must accept responsibility for the component's quality, evolution and maintenance. This component management role is crucial for reuse between projects within an organisation and is discussed in Chapter 8.

It must be noted that reuse requires investment. A reusable component by implication will (a) be more general and (b) have greater functionality than a component developed for a single project. The component must be very well documented. Reusable components are not produced by a single project unless it has wider objectives and more resources than it would have if it were just producing one information system. An objective of this volume is to describe the circumstances in which an organisation should make this investment.

4 Benefits, costs and risks

IS providers are under enormous pressure to increase the value for money provided by information systems and in particular:

- to develop new systems, for example to automate another area of business

- to enhance existing systems, for example to support new legislation.

The phrase *application backlog* is now commonly used in the government and commercial sectors to describe the situation when an organisation is unable to respond to these pressures.

Reuse is a powerful technique for avoiding or reducing this application backlog but it is not a panacea as there are costs and risks as well as benefits. It is however reasonable to ask why reuse has not been exploited for years if it offers such benefits. There are three reasons that reuse is more cost effective now than it was in the past:

- many of the pressures on IS providers are to reconfigure existing computer-based systems, typically replacing batch systems with on line transaction processing and a database management system, and not to computerise existing paper-based systems. The old computer-based system is a rich source of reusable components for the new one

- a range of new technologies are making reuse more technically feasible. These enabling technologies which include open systems, techniques of object-oriented programming and software tools are described in Chapter 6

- it is now recognised that reuse is a management as well as a technical issue. The principles of how to manage IS development with reuse are now quite well understood and are described in this volume.

Reuse, therefore, provides a powerful weapon in the IS provider's armoury. The remainder of this chapter itemises the benefits, costs and risks of reusing a component. Note that the production of a component for reuse also has associated benefits, costs and risks.

4.1 The benefits

The benefits of reuse are perhaps more obvious than its costs and risks and include:

- a faster delivery time. Reusing a component off the shelf is a lot quicker than developing a new component

- less development expertise is required by the project team so staff costs are reduced (although, as noted below, additional skills are needed in finding and adapting reusable components). For example, if a project reuses a database management system, an accounting package or a component which models taxpayers and their behaviour (see the examples above), then the project team does not need training in file access methods, accounting practices or personal tax allowances. Furthermore, this expertise is not needed during the system's development or its subsequent maintenance

- the implemented system should be more reliable by virtue of reusing tried and tested components

- reduced/maintenance costs. Ideally, a reusable component is maintained by its supplier in which case the project has no maintenance costs. Even if the project is responsible for the maintenance of reused components, the overall costs to the organisation are likely to be reduced because there are fewer components to be maintained

- a look and feel, common across the business, to systems built reusing the same user interface management system.

Historically, potential savings have been restricted by difficulties in tailoring and the costs which arise from the use of package solutions which contravene the organisation's existing strategy or policies, for example, the use of a particular database management system or third generation language.

Now, however, that a market is emerging for packages based on the ISO SQL standard and which use modern fourth generation languages or object-oriented languages, particularly C++, packages built using these tools are more portable and easier to tailor. Portability gives a wider market and hence should result in lower costs for the person reusing the component.

Reuse of analysis material leads to major savings during one of the most difficult stages of a project. It is easier for an analyst or user to extend existing models than to create them from scratch. For example, it is quite difficult to develop good data models. Analysts tend to get the core of the model of their area of interest right but produce a much weaker model around the edges where they have less business knowledge. Experience in many organisations shows that the provision of a corporate model at the beginning of a project can cut the analysis time significantly and reduce the risk of misunderstanding of interfaces.

4.2 The costs

The costs of reusing a component can include:

- searching for and evaluating a suitable reusable component. A project may wish to reuse a component for a certain part of the system. Finding the right component takes time and effort which must be planned for. Failure to allow adequate resources for this process may result in an inappropriate component being selected which is a source of costs and risks

- purchasing the reusable component. Often the producer of a reusable component receives the cost of producing the component by charging for each reuse of the component.

- adapting the reusable component to meet the particular requirements of the system where it is to be reused. The ease and, therefore, the cost of adapting a component varies considerably with the nature of the component and the extent to which it was designed to be adapted. The object-oriented paradigm in some circumstances is ideal for specialising a general purpose object class to meet particular requirements. On the other hand, the cost of extracting a code component which was not intended to be reused from an existing system and then adapting this code may be enormous (see reverse engineering, section 6.2)

- designing the system around the reusable component. Very often, it is impossible or impractical to adapt a reusable component, for example, the source code for a library of subroutines may not be available. If the component is to be reused then the interface of the system must be made to match that of the component, not vice versa. It is this possibility which makes it important to select reusable components as early in the project life-cycle as possible and so reduce the amount of redesign necessary

- reusing a component which does not match the organisation's IS strategy or policies. For example, the purchase of a package that does not use the organisation's preferred database management system may seriously impede attempts to share data between the new application and others. If the database management system does not use the organisation's preferred query language, for example SQL, then both the developers, who need to maintain the package, and the users, who wish to make ad hoc queries, need to acquire skills in the new query language

- costs associated with the additional skills which are needed to reuse components (see section 7.11) and to develop and maintain reusable components (see sections 8.5 to 8.7)

- purchase and establishment of a suitable library or repository to manage the reusable components.

4.3 The risks

The costs of reuse, described in the previous section are predictable in the sense that they can be realistically estimated. Reusing a component also has risks which are hard to estimate but which may result in very large costs. Too often, a project discovers these risks following bitter experience.

This section describes risks in three areas:

- maintenance
- quality
- legal issues.

Section 7.5 discusses how these risks may be managed. Normal risks associated with IS developments also apply but are not covered in this volume.

Maintenance

A project which reuses a component must recognise that the component needs support and maintenance, just as any other component of the system does. The possibility that support and maintenance are not available when needed constitutes a major risk.

There is no current consensus on how to manage libraries or repositories for reuse. There is very little experience apart from data definitions and program source code, most of this being for 'copy' reuse.

Quality

The quality of the component may be far below what the project's expectations were when the component was selected for reuse. For example, there may be more faults in the component which require more support and maintenance effort than was anticipated. If the component is extensively reused by an organisation then the risks to the organisation as a whole are proportionally greater.

Four particular risks associated with the quality of the component are that:

- the component may have unexpected non-functional characteristics which limit its utility. For example, the performance of the component may be inadequate or an apparently simple component may make large demands on machine resources, such as memory and disc space, because the simple component brings with it a large quantity of associated 'baggage'

- the documentation of the reusable component may not adequately describe it. The documentation may be inaccurate, incomplete or poorly written and structured. Any of these problems make the component very difficult to use

- a trusted system should be assembled from trusted components, that is components which assure the security and integrity of data which the system manages. There is a risk that a reusable component may not be dependable in this sense

- a number of techniques and methods for creating reusable components are still relatively immature eg reengineering, OO, formal methods.

Legal Issues

There are legal issues associated with the reuse of components. The European Directive on Software Protection and copyright law both give the component's developer substantial rights over its future use. In many circumstances, it is illegal to reuse a component developed for one system in another system without the consent of the component's developer.

Liability in the case of failure of the component may also constitute a risk. If a component is reused in a context for which it was not originally designed then the developer of the component is unlikely to be liable for its failure.

5 Reuse in application development

5.1 What do users want from information systems?

For most systems developed with methodologies such as SSADM users require a database to act as a simulation of what is happening in their business. They can then use information from the database to support decisions to be applied to the real world of the business. It is easier and more effective to obtain information from the simulation than to deal directly with the real world.

For example, in EU-Rent (EU-Rent is a car rentals case study developed by CCTA for illustration of some SSADM enhancements. It is described in more detail in the ISE Library volume on Distributed Systems: Application Development.) when a customer wants to reserve a car, an EU-Rent booking clerk will check the car-rentals file and link a car record to the customer record in the database. This is easier (and probably more reliable) than walking around the car park to see which cars are available, and sticking a label on one saying 'Reserved for Mr. Smith'. But the decision made in the database leads to real-world action - a real customer gets a real car and will drive it away, bring it back and pay for the rental (see Figure 1).

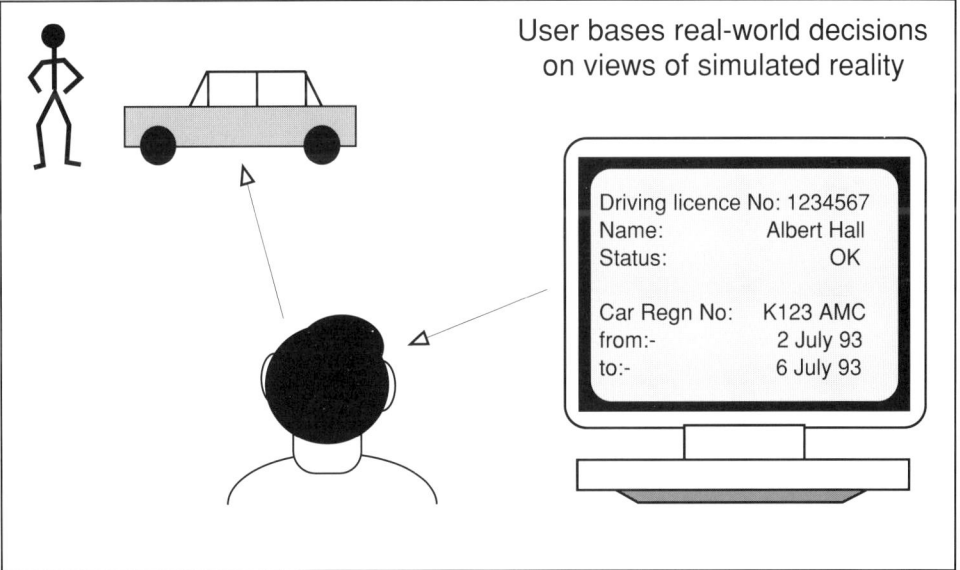

Figure 1: Real world and simulated reality

Users do not want the entirety of their business to be simulated. Many aspects of the real world are not relevant to the business activities that need information support. We determine the scope of an IT system by:

- agreeing the set of business activities to be supported. These are real-world activities. In EU-Rent they would include: making sure there are enough cars available to fill the next day's rentals, moving cars from one branch to another, allocating specific cars to rental reservations, deciding whether to blacklist an unreliable customer, and so on. How we describe these activities may be outside the scope of the IT development methodology (as is the case with SSADM), but we must have a clear understanding of what the business activities are

- defining what support users need from the IT system. We define functional requirements by developing detail for two aspects of this:

    - defining what information is needed to support each business activity

    - deciding whether any business activities can be wholly or partially automated. In EU-Rent, for example, the automated system might allocate specific cars to reservations when there are cars of the requested group available at the branch, and refer the problem to the booking clerk when there are not. The booking clerk could then decide whether to offer an upgrade, arrange for the customer to be taken to another branch, and so on.

5.2 A conceptual schema for information support

The scope of the required IT system is defined by the information support needed for the business (see Figure 2).

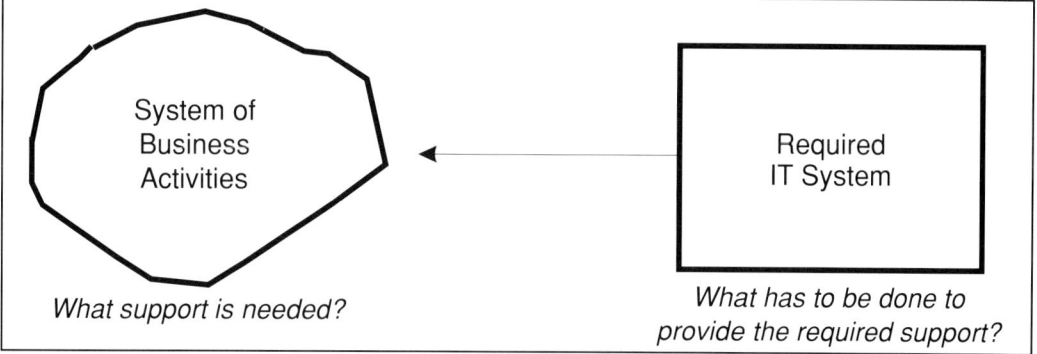

Figure 2: Scope of required system

In most IT development methodologies we specify the provision of information support by:

- developing a logical data model from the entities and relationships within the scope of the business activities. We shall, eventually, turn the logical data model into a database that will simulate the behaviour of those entities and relationships

- testing the logical data model for capability of providing information support; we would usually document the access paths that describe how the required outputs can be extracted from the logical data model.

We can build up the attributes of the logical data model entities as a result of this validation, either informally (by asking for each entity as we develop an access path, 'what attributes would be needed to support this output') or formally, using relational data analysis on the output specifications.

For the logical data model to provide useful information support, it must be kept up to date (see Figure 3). Updates of the data model simulate or record events in the business; we need to identify the business events that have to be captured. In EU-Rent they would include rental reservation, collection of car by customer, return of car from rental, car service, car write-off.

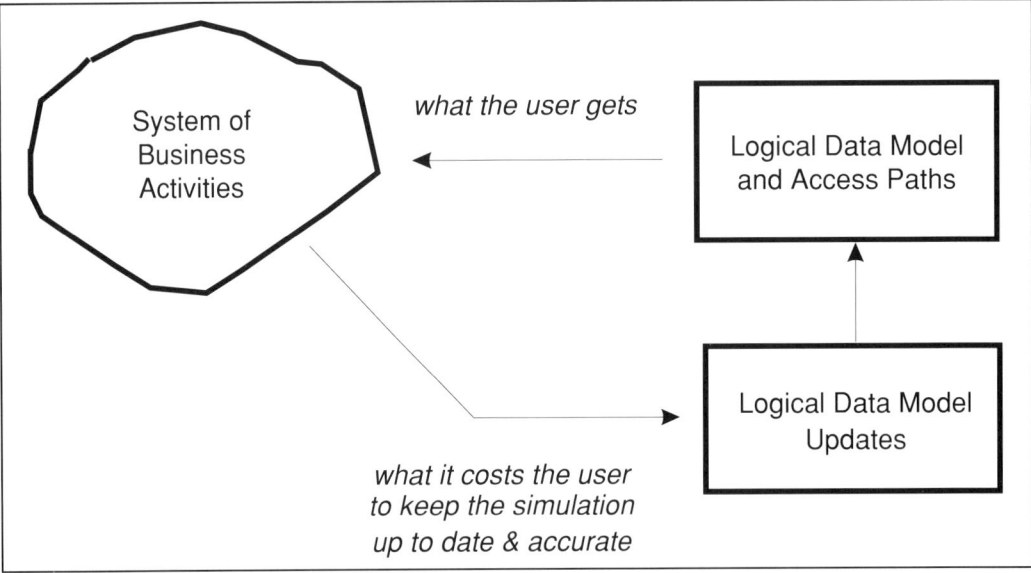

Figure 3: Keeping the logical data model up to date

If we know what has to be in the data model (to provide the outputs needed to support the business activities), we can find out what events are needed to keep it up to date, by analysing its entities, attributes and relationships. There must be events for:

- birth and death of every entity type
- swapping of changeable relationships
- making and breaking of optional relationships
- changing every changeable attribute
- imposing and removing constraints by setting states of entities.

We must then ensure that input is available for every type of event identified, and find out where in the business it comes from.

This part of the system description - logical data model, provision of information support to business activities, and the inputs needed to keep the model up-to-date - we call the **Conceptual Schema**. It defines the scope of the IT system. We develop it by a process of **discovery** - by finding out what information is needed to support business activities, how it can be provided from the logical data model, what is needed to keep the logical data model up to date, where we can obtain the inputs.

5.3 A 3-schema specification architecture

We also have to be concerned with an **External Schema**, that determines how users can access the system, and an **Internal Schema**, that maps the logical data model on to an implementation technology and provides access to the stored data (see Figure 4).

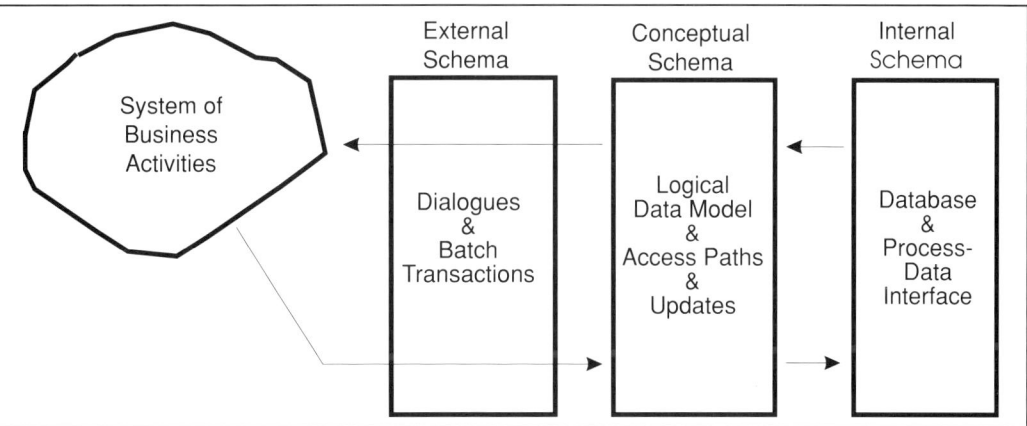

Figure 4: 3-schema specification architecture

External schema   The external schema is defined in functions; they support users in carrying out business activities, and are implemented in (either or both of):

- dialogues within menus

- the batch input-output subsystem.

The external schema passes event data and enquiry triggers to the conceptual schema, and receives event and enquiry output in response. It has three major elements:

- a packaging of the outputs provided by and inputs needed by the conceptual schema, into functions that serve user roles

- processing:

    - to convert inputs from business activities to event data and enquiry triggers

    - to convert event and enquiry responses to outputs for users

    - to detect and diagnose syntactic errors

    - to report semantic errors notified by processes in the conceptual schema

    - to maintain and manipulate transient data

    - to navigate between the elements of a function and between functions

- a mapping of the external schema logical specification to a user interface technology.

The external schema differs from the conceptual schema in two significant ways:

- it is developed by design and engineering, not by discovery

- there could be several different external designs for a single conceptual schema.

Design versus discovery

For the conceptual schema there is, within fairly narrow boundaries, a 'right' answer based on a data model that simulates the business entities and relationships to some required level of precision and currency. It is kept up to date by simulating business behaviour - by modelling events and updating the data model. We can properly call it a **conceptual model** that simulates the business activity.

There is no 'right' answer to be discovered for an external schema. There are many factors outside the designer's control - allocation of user responsibilities within the business, level of ability and training of users, constraints on technology to be used, interface style guides, arbitrary rules and preferences, legislation. The designer has to make trade-offs between conflicting requirements and constraints and construct a workable external design acceptable to all users. We should call it an external **design**.

Multiple external designs for a single conceptual schema

There could be several external designs for the same conceptual model. This is obviously true at the interface technology level. More-or-less the same functions could be delivered via, for example, Motif, MS Windows, text menus, SQL-supported forms or batch input/output. A system supporting different types of workstation could include several interfaces concurrently.

But the differences could be more fundamental. The information support provided by a conceptual model could be packaged in different ways into functions, to serve different organisational structures and user roles. (see Figure 5)

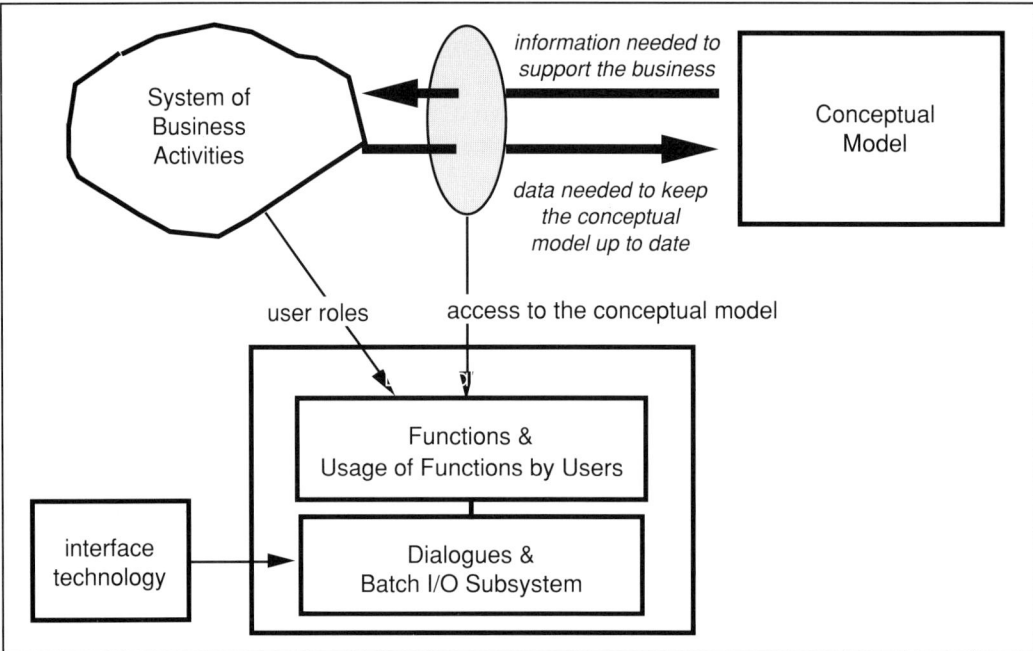

Figure 5: Multiple external designs for a single conceptual schema

The Inland Revenue uses this approach in allocating responsibilities in local offices. Different IR local offices do the same range of business activities, but local managers can allocate them, and the IT services that support them, to their staff in different ways. The packaging of IT services varies from office to office.

Internal Schema

The internal schema is also a designed system; there could be several internal designs for the same conceptual model (see Figure 6). There are many data management platforms available to implement a conceptual model, and many ways to use their facilities to meet the physical system objectives.

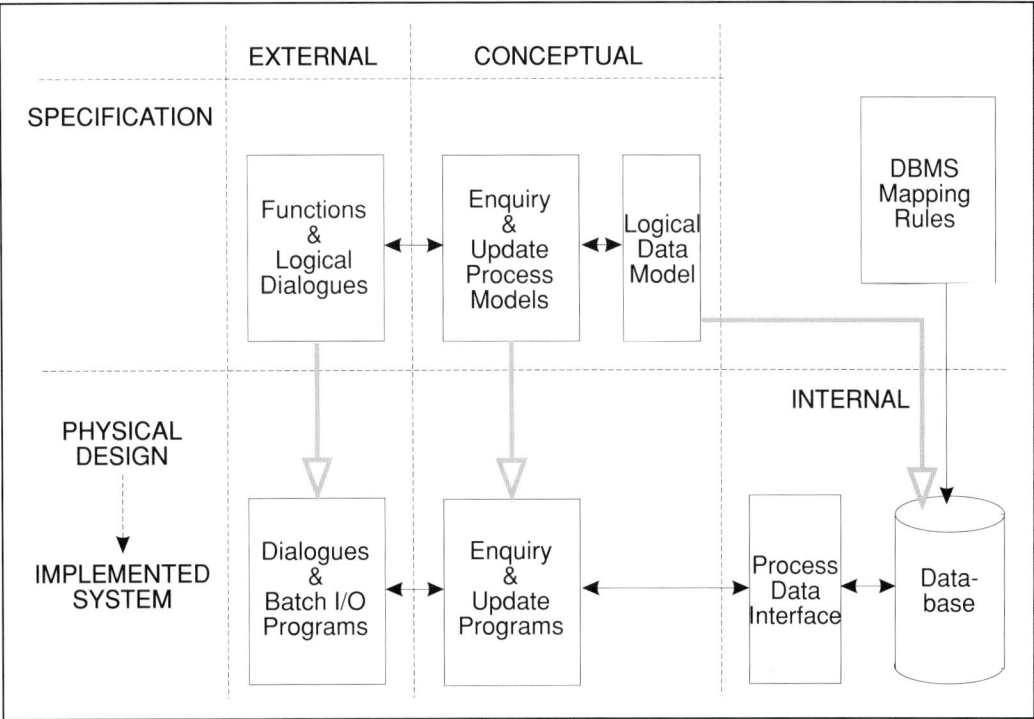

Figure 6: Conceptual model/internal design relationship

In a distributed system the same data model (or submodel) could be implemented (with replicated or partitioned instance data) at different locations, using different DBMSs and different types of hardware.

Each schema is implemented

Code is produced for components in each schema. For example, a major European bank uses SSADM and the 3-schema specification architecture. The bank has developed a default standard that processes in the conceptual model (SSADM update and enquiry process models) are coded in C; embedded SQL/2 acts as the program-data interface. Some enquiries are coded from enquiry access paths rather than full enquiry process models.

Then, the external design can be implemented in any dialogue manager(s) that can make C calls; the internal design can be implemented with any DBMS that can be accessed with SQL/2. In practice there is some DBMS product-specific optimisation of code, especially for database access (some proprietary extensions of SQL/2 provide significant performance improvements) but the separation of components in the 3-schema architecture is strongly encouraged.

5.4 Reuse in the 3-schema specification architecture

There are many opportunities for reuse of components in the 3-schema specification architecture, as will now be shown.

Conceptual model services to support different business activities

The IT services in the conceptual model are:

- enquiries to support business activities

- automated execution of business activities

- updates to record data needed to support business activities.

Some services may support more than one type of business activity. For example, in EU-Rent, the enquiry on availability of cars in a given rental group can support a booking clerk allocating a car to a rental reservation or a manager redistributing cars between rental branches.

Conceptual model services with different data storage technologies

The services in the conceptual model can be used with different DBMSs; only the program-data interface needs to be changed.

Functions with different user interface technologies

A function is a packaging of conceptual model services to support a business activity carried out by a user. For example, in EU-Rent, a booking clerk handling a walk-in rental needs:

- to check that there is a suitable car available

- to check that the customer is not on the blacklist

- to assign the car to the customer and complete the details of the rental contract.

The same function can be implemented with different interface technologies, eg in a text dialogue, or in a GUI such as MS Windows or Motif.

Conceptual model with different user organisation structures

Events and enquiries in the conceptual model may be packaged into functions in different ways, to support different user roles. For example, the EU-Rent conceptual model defines the IT services to support a car rental business. It could be used for other car rental companies (provided that they carry out the same business activities as EU-Rent) with different management structures and user roles.

Different levels of reuse

Reuse of the conceptual model as described above can be at the level of:

- requirements, that could be used to specify conceptual models with different levels of precision (eg degree to which data is summarised, degree to which events are generalised), and different boundaries of automation (ie which business activities are to be automated)

- specifications, that could be coded in different languages

- coded modules, that could be used with different dialogues and different DBMSs.

Mapping of 3-schema components on to technical architectures

Components can be mapped on to different technical architectures. For example, in a distributed system, external and conceptual components could be implemented together providing a complete application at the workstation with remote database calls to the stored data (see Figure 7).

Alternatively, the external design could be implemented at the workstation with remote calls of event and enquiry procedures stored with the data. This is the simple client-server model that several DBMS vendors offer (see Figure 7).

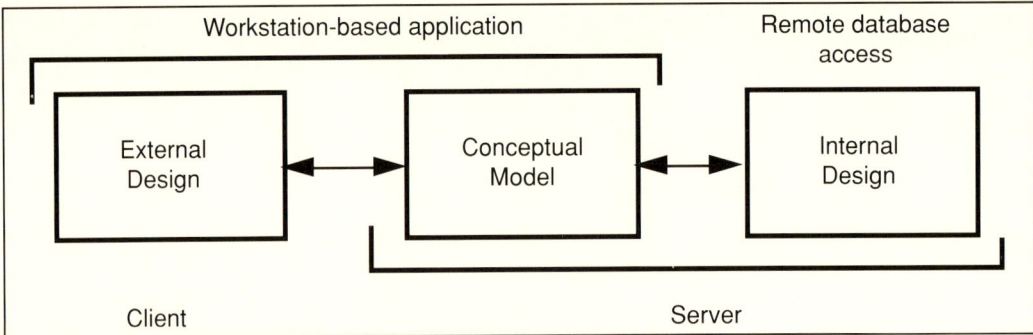

Figure 7: Mapping of components to technical architectures

> These types of mapping could be done for coded components, but are more likely to be done for specifications so that optimisation of data access and communications are possible within the selected architecture.

Presentation of external design

> Mapping of functions to a user interface technology needs to be supported by an application style guide. Parts of the style guide can be provided in a component library; for example:
>
> - log-on/off dialogue
>
> - skeletons or templates for menu screen or window
>
> - support for dedicated function keys (help, print hard copy, abandon dialogue etc.)
>
> - help text
>
> - GUI 'widgets' (buttons, icons, pop-up windows etc.).
>
> Such libraries, as well as preserving the dialogue 'look and feel' promoted by the style guide, enable the designer and programmer to work at a higher level than the implementation language. They can work faster, using tested components, with many of the mundane decisions on design and format already made for them.

5.5 Types of reuse within SSADM

Many software development and many software maintenance projects use SSADM. This section explains the circumstances in which reuse can be exploited and reusable components can be created in such projects.

Reuse can occur:

- within a project as part of step wise development or perfective maintenance (eg development to enhance an existing system)

- in a project which is building a replacement system in the same business area as the old system

- in a project in a different business area of the same organisation

- in a project in a different business area in a different organisation

- in a project in the same business area of a different organisation

- across different organisations.

Reuse during step wise development

Some projects are planned to develop in a step wise manner. Some perfective maintenance work is really the addition of new functionality and is treated as step wise development in this volume. In some organisations, the majority of software development is done step wise.

Each cycle of step wise development must go through the thought processes of the complete SSADM lifecycle. The analyst requires considerable skill to decide which steps need substantial documentation effort and which to carry out in the mind. The ideal is to make each iteration in a few days or weeks. But the specification is not what is on paper but what is in the CASE tool. Each cycle of refinement is not reusing paper (used for agreement) but reusing design decisions made to reach the agreement. At each iteration, the analyst must develop a new version of

		the documentation to reflect the changes made to the analysis of requirements and the system design.
Reuse during a replacement project		A replacement project reuses all available SSADM documentation in the same way as an incremental development project. The distinction is that a project is usually thought of as a replacement if consideration is to be given to new business system options or a new logical design.
Reuse in a different business area		SSADM deliverables from one business area are reusable in a different business area when there is some similarity between them. The recommended approach to finding similar components is to look for shared or similar entities. For further information see the *Corporate Data Modelling* volume of the *Information Management Library*. The functional and behavioural aspects of a component are then assessed from its association with the entities. In general, there may be reusable components if the two business areas have one or more entities in common.
Reuse of components developed by other organisations		For application software components, an organisation should strive to use components from other organisations provided they are documented according to SSADM standards. It must of course be easier and cheaper for the organisation to integrate the reusable component with its own SSADM designed components, than to develop a new component of the required quality. Effective, efficient and economical maintenance has to be available.
		Most system software is designed for reuse. System software should be used only as specified in the supplier's manuals, otherwise the user risks lock in to unsupported facilities.
5.6	**What is an SSADM reusable component**	Each of the products from an SSADM life-cycle is potentially reusable. For example, the logical data model consisting of the logical data structure diagram, the entity descriptions and the relationship descriptions developed during one project could be a very valuable

input to a new project in the same business area (see figure 8).

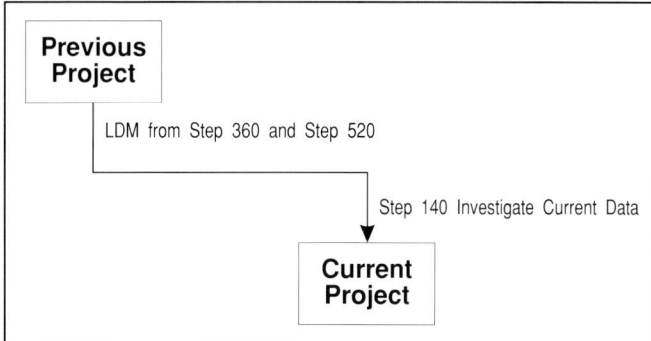

Figure 8: Example flow of a reusable component between projects

To facilitate reuse the SSADM analysis or design steps concerned should be thorough and the results quality assured. The products of these steps should be checked for consistency with the corporate data models and other architectural rules into which they fit.

If products early in the life-cycle can be reused, it is likely that the products later in the life-cycle can also be reused, particularly if the target environment is the same or similar. Reuse of such products is less likely if the target environment is radically different. For example, the business requirements, data flows, logical data model, entity event model and function models for an accounting system may be the same, but the physical design will be radically different, if the first project was a batch system using conventional files and the new system is to run under Windows and be based on relational database technology.

The size of SSADM product to be reused will vary. For example, a whole system from requirements to implementation may be adopted. Alternatively, a group of entities and their functions covering an area such as the management of employees and jobs might be reused by a project sharing a common personnel database with another system. At the lowest level, a code table or a single attribute definition might be shared.

The importance of the reuse of even small components should not be under-emphasised. Every time a code table is re-used, an interface problem between two systems is avoided and the development of two or three data entry dialogues is saved. Every time an entity and its associated event handling is shared, a significant amount of business analysis, design and implementation is saved.

Note that a useful medium sized reusable component is often a group of entities and their associated events and functionality. In the Inland Revenue, this concept is termed a Corporate Logical Unit of Manageable Proportions (CLUMP). As a CLUMP encapsulates business and implementation knowledge, the project reusing it does not have to gain a deep business understanding in that area or an understanding of the implementation.

5.7 Tailoring SSADM for reuse

Further discussion on SSDAM support for reuse and an example of tailoring the method to support reuse are given in Annex A.

6 Enabling methods and technologies

The ability to reuse components between projects is enhanced by a range of technologies which are summarised in this chapter. Some of these technologies are mature and are familiar to managers in many organisations. Others are not yet widely used but will have a large impact on reuse practice as they mature.

This chapter explains how and why these technologies facilitate reuse. The objective is to encourage senior managers to adopt the mature technologies and prepare their staff for the arrival of technologies which are not yet mature.

6.1 Design methods

Structured methods

The acceptance of structured methods, particularly SSADM, has meant that designers of complex information systems use the same vocabulary and the same techniques. It was difficult to identify common components between systems before the advent of structured methods, because the same component might have been described in completely different ways. See also Chapter 5 and Annex A.

With the widespread acceptance of SSADM, the library of reusable components can be structured according to the type of the components, for example as entities and dialogue structures.

Domain analysis

Domain analysis is a process by which the knowledge used to develop IS's in a particular business area (domain) is identified, captured and organised so that it can be reused to create a new IS. This analysis involves constructing a coherent model of existing systems as well as current and future requirements.

Domain analysis, which is focused on reuse, comprises the following steps which recur repeatedly for different kinds of component:

- identification of reusable entities

- abstraction or generalisation

- classification and cataloguing for further reuse.

Domain analysis is a new technique and there is some debate about how the domain model should be structured. It has, however, been used successfully by some commercial organisations and provides an approach for the Inter-Project Board (see Chapter 9) to evolve a broad but shallow view of the projects it co-ordinates.

Object-oriented methods All structured methods, including SSADM, help to make reuse a possibility. Object-oriented methods have two features which are particularly valuable for component reuse:

- encapsulation

- inheritance.

Encapsulation The analysis, design and implementation of a system using object-oriented methods is based on the concept of objects, each of which has a state and a behaviour, which co-operate to provide the system functionality. Each object has a well defined interface while the implementation of the object, that is how the state is represented and how the behaviour is achieved, is hidden to other objects in the system.

An object is thus an encapsulated, self-contained part of the system which has the potential to be reused in other contexts. Furthermore, the entire project life-cycle is centred on objects so it is easy and natural to trace the initial specification of an object during analysis through to its implementation.

Inheritance Each object is an instance of a class, for example Fred Smith is an instance of the class of all taxpayers. Classes are organised in a hierarchy, for example Figure 9 shows that taxpayers are either married or single. Many properties of taxpayers are common to both married and single people. Such properties are therefore associated with the Taxpayer class and are inherited by the subclasses Married Taxpayer and Single Taxpayer. The two subclasses have additional properties which are special to married or single people.

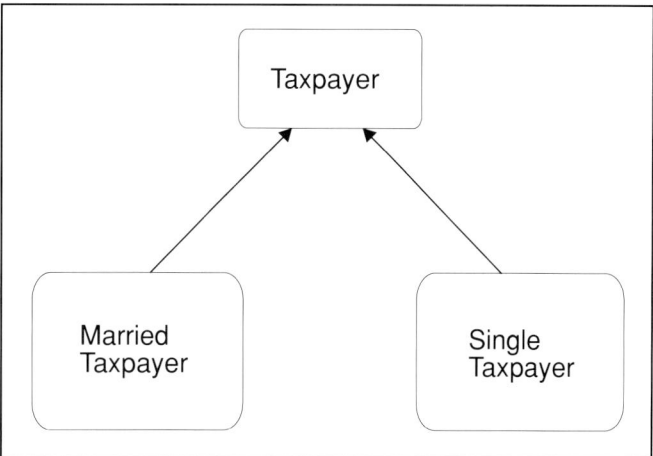

Figure 9: **An example class hierarchy**

This approach provides a very economical way of describing objects. It also supports the Open-Closed principle that each class is:

- closed in the sense that it provides the services defined by its interface, and that interface is immutable

- open in the sense that a new subclass can be defined to meet new or changing requirements. For example, if new legislation means that divorced people have different tax assessments then a new subclass could be added to the Single Taxpayer class from which it would inherit most of its properties.

The Open-Closed principle is very valuable for reuse. Because a class is closed, the user of a reusable component can be confident that the class will not change. Because the class is open, the user will be able to adapt this class to meet special requirements.

Caveats	Although object-orientation has many merits, especially for component reuse, there are two important caveats. First, it should be recognised that object-oriented methods are immature. Secondly, object-orientation is not a panacea; although it provides approaches to some of the technical issues associated with reuse it has little to say on the management issues which are at least as important and are the subject of much of this volume.
Formal methods	Formal methods comprise mathematically precise notations for describing components of an information system and techniques for proving that an implementation of a component is correct with respect to its specification. Z and VDM are the most widely known and used formal notations.

Formal methods have the potential to improve reuse for the following reasons:

- a formal description of a component provides a developer with an exact description of what the component does

- the formal description of a component can be used by an automated tool to search for a component with required properties

- if the implementation of a formally specified component has been proven to be correct then the quality of the component is guaranteed.

In practice, it must be recognised that formal methods are in their infancy. The use of formal methods requires highly developed mathematical skill and is very time consuming. Not all properties of components are easy to describe formally. For these reasons, formal methods are a technology for the future rather than a technique which should now be widely adopted to develop information systems.

6.2 Reverse engineering

Most medium to large organisations already have large computer based systems which, despite their limitations and imperfections, are tried and tested.

These systems are potentially an enormous asset to developers of new systems because they contain software components which could be reused.

Unfortunately, in practice, it is often very difficult to extract reusable components from existing systems. Many old systems were not designed using SSADM and are poorly structured. For many operational systems there is no reliable documentation of the system's structure. The only way to find out how the system works is to look at the code.

Organisations are faced with the problem of abstracting the structure of a system as potentially reusable components. This process is often called reverse engineering because it passes backwards through the conventional life-cycle from implementation to design. The process is also sometimes called re-documentation or design recovery.

Tools have been available for many years which build cross reference tables showing how procedures, functions or subroutines or modules, call other procedures but this is only part of the problem and does not capture the meaning of the procedural code. Tools are starting to emerge, for example, from the IED research project RECAST, which help with the extraction of SSADM products from unstructured COBOL.

The most successful reverse engineering tools are those which extract the data structures, that is entities and relationships, from data declarations in code, for example from COBOL data divisions. These tools recognise that an expert user is needed to steer the tool towards the correct interpretation of the code.

Reverse engineering is the subject of much research and development activity both in industry and in the academic community, for example, the IED research project RECAST and the EC funded ESPRIT projects REBOOT, REDO, PRACTITIONER and SCALE. This activity is evidence of both the importance of reuse and of the immaturity of existing methods and tools.

To summarise, organisations should recognise the value of the assets which are embedded in their existing systems, but must also recognise the cost and difficulty of extracting these assets as reusable components. Software tools have an important role in reverse engineering but the role of the expert, who understands the system, what it does and how it works, is at least as significant.

6.3 Repository technology

The store of reusable components is called the component library or the repository. The repository provides facilities for managing a component through its life-cycle including inserting the component in the library, finding a component in the library and managing changes to library components. The facilities which a repository provides should be standardised so that it can be used by diverse people and tools.

The requirements for a repository include those of a conventional database, for example, security, integrity, multi-user access. A repository has additional requirements in the following areas:

- **configuration management**. For example, the repository must provide version control, must allow complex components with complex inter-relationships to be stored, and must support long transactions

- **data dictionary facilities**. The repository must know about the different types of reusable components and the relationships between them. For example entities, attributes, processes, dialogue designs.

The repository may also have to recognise the differences between conceptual, external and internal components. It may be simpler and more effective to use a number of different libraries for each of the various types of components.

There are potentially three major problems with libraries:

- there is very little experience of using them for anything other than code. Even the use of corporate data models as libraries for data specifications has had a mixed history. Whether libraries will work as envisaged for other types of component is not known: some practical feedback is needed.

- if tailoring reuse is widely-practised, many versions of a reusable component can be created with narrower application than the original. Adding tailored versions back into the library needs careful management, for three reasons:

  - because they are more specialised, their reusability is reduced and there is likely to be less return on the overhead of managing them in the library

  - as more changes are overlaid on a component, it will become more difficult to maintain, and less likely to be reusable for further tailoring

  - the library may become cluttered with components of low reusability, with perhaps many variants on a theme, and finding the required components becomes so difficult that developers will not use the library.

  (Note: It is possible that tailoring reuse will be better supported in OO environments, if tailoring is done by adding subclasses to existing superclasses, leaving the originals unchanged. However, this technology is immature for databases, and most of the readers of this guide will not be using object databases in the next two or three years.)

  (Note: OO programming environments such as MacApp, that provide class libraries, generally assume that components will be copied out and modified if necessary, but the modified copies will not be put back into the library).

- library searching criteria are not well-defined, except around the conceptual model ('Where is this entity/attribute used?'). How do we organise business rules, user roles, constraints, functional and non-functional requirements, functions, dialogue structures, enquiries.....etc so that developers can find what is useful? Informal browsing will work only for small libraries. The real benefits of reuse will come as libraries get bigger and richer. This is an area that needs further research and feedback from experience.

Some of the approaches which may lead to the provision of suitable repository facilities are described below.

IRDS standards

Information Resource Dictionary System (IRDS) standards concentrate on the data dictionary facilities which must be provided by the repository. In 1988, an IRDS standard was approved by the American National Standards Institute (ANSI). Since then, emphasis has switched to a different IRDS standard from ISO (the International Standards Organization) which has recently been supported by ANSI.

ISO IRDS supports a set of content standards which define standard data structures at two levels:

- Definition Level standards - data structures required by methods and tools, for example, for entities, processes and dialogue designs

- Domain level standards - data structures required by specific business areas; these domain standards are defined in terms of definition level standards.

Recently ANSI has announced its intention to back PCTE as the standard for enterprise repositories, leaving the UK as the sole promoter of IRDS. The future of IRDS therefore is in some doubt.

IBM AD/Cycle	The IBM repository lies at the heart of AD/Cycle: IBM's framework for IS development tools. IBM has recently published specifications for access to the repository and for the data which the repository contains, and these specifications have been offered to ANSI as standards. If the specifications are accepted by standard bodies and by tool suppliers, then the IBM repository could be of great importance for component reuse. At this stage however, it is not possible to predict the level of future acceptance.
PCTE	Portable Common Tools Environment (PCTE) is a platform for IS development tools. PCTE provides excellent facilities for storing CASE tool data and for configuration management but provides nothing analogous to the IRDS Content Standards. The PCTE philosophy is that it is up to CASE tool suppliers to agree among themselves how components are represented in the PCTE repository. See the CCTA ISE Library volume *PCTE an Overview*. PCTE is currently a European Computer Manufacturer's Association (ECMA) standard and is proposed as an ISO standard. There are commercial implementations of PCTE but these are not yet widely used.
Proprietary repositories and current best practice	The IBM repository is a proprietary system which is not yet widely used but is likely to influence repository standards. Current best practice, both within and outside government, is to use proprietary repositories to hold data from CASE tools. Such repositories include ICL's DDS, Digital's Cohesion environment with the Digital CDD repository at its core, the Oracle CASE Dictionary, the Excelerator data dictionary and the Maestro II OMS. These repositories provide varying support for configuration management. Many repositories provide facilities for exporting and reimporting the data they contain. However, a translation process is needed to move data between them and CASE tools because

repositories use different data structures. There are tools, for example Exchange from Software One, which automate this translation for the repositories and tools which they support. Before the advent of standard repositories, organisations should make use of these pragmatic tools to reuse design components held in different proprietary repositories.

6.4 Open systems

An important benefit of open systems is that they enable the reuse of components between systems. As illustrated in Figure 10 open systems allow components to:

- be portable between platforms

- co-operate even though the components are distributed between platforms

- share data structures and the data

- have a common look and feel.

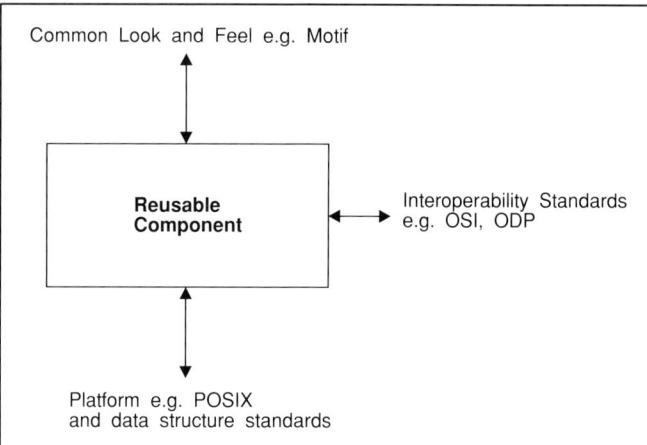

Figure 10: Reuse and open systems

Open systems are achieved by the adoption of standards. This chapter summarises the most important open system standards for reuse and highlights their maturity or immaturity. The advantage of open standards is that an organisation can select from a wide variety of suppliers.

Chapter 6
Enabling methods and technologies

The special case of repository standards, which are of particular importance for reuse during system development, is discussed above.

Portability

If a reusable component is to be reused in several environments, the component must be portable between these environments. There are several aspects to component portability:

- **user interface**. Standardisation of the user interface means that the user interfaces provided by components all have a similar look and feel. The standards in this area include X Windows and Microsoft Windows

- **languages**. There are now established standards for many commonly used languages including COBOL, C, Pascal and FORTRAN, and SQL. These standards allow, or at least help, software which complies with the standard to be reused on many platforms and should be adopted wherever possible. There are no open standards for fourth-generation languages (4GLs)

- **tools**. Given the absence of standards for 4GLs, an organisation should consider restricting the variety of database management systems and CASE tools which it uses. Components are then reusable between projects which use the same tools. However, this approach risks locking the organisation into a single supplier and may contravene EC legislation. The long term solution to this problem is provided by repository standards (see above) and proposed future developments to the database language SQL

- **operating system**. Any system must make use of the services provided by the operating system platform either directly or via middleware such as a database management system. A component which uses operating system services directly can only be reused by systems which run on that operating system. An organisation should use

	standardised operating system facilities as defined by, for example, POSIX or XPG3.
Interoperability	OSI standards, in particular the government OSI profile (GOSIP), allow a component in one place to communicate and co-operate with a component in another. Components can therefore in principle be reused across a network.
	More recent initiatives build on the OSI communication standards by defining the protocol by which one component uses the services provided by another. For example, DCE (Distributed Computing Environment) is now a relatively mature technology for invoking distributed procedures. Future standards for Open Distributed Processing and Object Management will further facilitate the reuse of distributed IS components.
	Limited interoperability can be achieved through the use of distributed database technology and Remote Database Access (RDA).
Data structures	There is increasing standardisation of data structures for representing different kinds of business information. Examples of such standards include:

- Electronic Data Interchange (EDI) standards which define structures for a wide range of business data including personnel data, orders, quotations, invoices and inventory data. Both the United Nations and the European Community have been instrumental in establishing EDI standards for specific industry sectors

- the Open Document Architecture (ODA) standard defines the basic structure in text which may be sent by OSI systems. It allows a mixture of text and graphics to be contained in the document

- Standardisation Agreements (STANAGs) between NATO countries allow the communication of defence related information between NATO forces |

- the Data Coordinating Group (DCG) is an International Standards Organisation (ISO) sponsored group which seeks to standardise data elements in diverse application sectors including eg, health, libraries, trade.

It should be clear to the reader that there is a wide range of competing and overlapping standards for application data structures. Despite this complexity, the potential benefits of standardisation are such that senior IS managers and the intelligent customer of IS services should stay informed of standards initiatives and adopt appropriate standards as they mature and are approved.

7 Planning for reuse

7.1 Key messages

It is well worth while repeating the key messages of this volume at this point. They are:

- We might get more for our money: there are benefits in reusing existing components rather than developing new ones - cost, development time, testing, robustness

- Nothing comes free: there are overheads in specifying, designing and building reusable components, and keeping them in accessible libraries

- Reusability can happen by intent or by accident: we should plan for intended reuse and regard accidental reusability as a bonus

- Sometimes we get it wrong: the overheads of creating and maintaining some components that we hoped would be reusable turn out to be not worth the benefit we get from them. This should not make us give up, but we have to manage the trade-off.

- Reuse can happen at several levels: requirements, specifications, designs, code. Almost all the real experience is in two areas:

    - code

    - copying of data specifications from corporate data models.

7.2 Getting started

It is not recommended that an organisation should immediately establish new organisational roles, mandate new approaches to IS development and invest in the development of new reusable components. Progress to high levels of reuse within an organisation should be gradual.

The first step towards reuse at levels 3 and 4 should be to initiate a pilot project which gives the organisation practical experience of reuse. This experience lets managers establish the roles and approaches appropriate for their particular organisation. A successful pilot project is also the first step in winning the hearts and minds of the IS developers or those responsible for specifying IS development services, whose commitment is essential to the success of reuse.

The pilot project should:

- be staffed by professionals who are sympathetic to reuse and who do not see reuse as a threat to their professional skills. The project manager should be committed to the success of the pilot

- be of a reasonable size, comparable with that of other projects in the organisation. Reuse by a small project establishes little

- not be critical for the organisation, because there is a risk associated with the take-up of any new approach to IS development. Conversely, the project should be visible within the organisation so that its lessons and successes are publicised

- reuse components developed by other projects in the same organisation. To do so effectively, the pilot must have the cooperation of the developers of the components to be reused.

The success of the pilot should be monitored. Careful records should be kept of which components were reused and how these components were adapted. At the end of the pilot, a comparison should be made between the cost of the project and an estimate of the cost if components had not been reused.

When reviewing this bottom line, it should be recognised that, as a by-product, the pilot project may have adapted existing components which will be suitable for reuse by subsequent projects. This adaption, coupled with the lessons learnt from the pilot, means that reuse by subsequent projects may be even more beneficial.

7.3 Who decides

The decision whether a project should reuse an existing component or design a component for reuse may be either:

- imposed on a project by a higher authority, for example the Inter-Project Board (described in Chapter 9) or the Programme Board

- made by the Project Board

- made by the Project Manager and individual members of the development team (in which case authorization from the Project Board may well be needed).

In general, it is likely that a higher authority, such as the Programme Board, will be responsible for the design and or specification of reusable components and the reuse of:

- large, strategic components that are built in house

- large components that are bought in for general use

- components that will become standard for all systems

- components required to achieve integration between projects.

Conversely a project more usually identifies opportunities for reuse that are smaller and less strategic. However, projects and individual project team members should be encouraged to design for reuse and wherever appropriate to reuse all types of component at all stages of the life-cycle.

Project managers should be given clear direction concerning the degree to which they can reuse without reference to their Project Board. For example, they may be authorised to use any component held in the component library without any bureaucracy other than to record the fact that they have used that component.

A project should always reuse previous analysis and design work carried out in the same business area. In projects carrying out maintenance or adopting an incremental approach to development, reuse of existing analysis and design must become the normal way of working.

7.4 Deciding whether to reuse

Designing for reuse

Where it is likely that a system component from any stage of the life-cycle may have common applicability across the organisation or business area, then designing for reuse should be considered.

A component which has been designed for reuse will by implication be more generalised and in the case of a code element will be parameter driven, rather than have application specific elements embedded. This means that it will be more expensive to develop as possibly more extensive analysis will be needed together with more complex application development. However once the component has been developed, the costs of subsequent reuse should be much lower, as less or even no tailoring will be required.

Reuse of large strategic components

Decisions concerning whether to reuse large strategic components may be taken during the development of the programme plan or may originate within the project, for example, when a package solution is proposed.

The Project Board of a project that will use a reusable component will ratify the decision during the early stages of the project. The decision will be reviewed by the project team during an SSADM Feasibility Study at step 030 and during Requirements Analysis at steps 210 and 220 (Business Systems Options). The degree to which a project will evaluate whether to use a reusable component should be defined in the Project Initiation Document.

Sometimes the use of existing functionality or data is part of an overall strategy or policy which the project should not spend effort re-examining. On other occasions the decision may be finely balanced and the criteria discussed later should be applied.

Reuse of smaller components	Decisions concerning when to reuse smaller components are taken within the project. Where the components are items of program code or particular data structures where the data is not shared between items of software, the decisions may be made during SSADM Stages 5 (Logical Design) and 6 (Physical Design).
Criteria for the decision	The decision whether to reuse a candidate reusable component must be based on a comparison of the costs of reuse with the costs of the initial development and maintenance. Of course the rigour and formality of this comparison process depends on the size and value of the candidate reusable component.

The costs of initial development and maintenance should be estimated by conventional estimating techniques such as function point analysis, or by comparison with past experience.

It is much harder to estimate the cost of reuse. Industry experience of reuse is less than of initial development. There are very many types of reuse, depending on factors such as whether:

- the component has been designed for reuse
- reuse is:
    - between projects within one organisation
    - between organisations
    - from a third party supplier
- the component is maintained by its developer, by a central library management function or by its user

- library management tools are used.

In general, reuse involves the following costs, not all of which are applicable in all circumstances:

- design of, development and testing of a reusable component

- time spent searching for, and perhaps not finding, a candidate reusable component

- evaluating the candidate reusable component to determine whether it meets, or could meet, the needs of the new system

- purchasing the reusable component from its supplier

- reverse engineering a reusable component from an existing system

- adapting the reusable component to meet the particular requirements of the new system

- adjusting the design of the new system so that the reusable component can be effectively reused

- maintaining the reusable component.

When estimating the cost of reuse, consider:

- that reuse is most beneficial in those areas which are not related to the organisation's core business. For example, a government department should not develop a database management system

- the implications of reusing a component if the supplier of the component has no interest in its successful reuse and therefore provides no support

- that the cost of reactively reverse engineering a component which was not designed to be reused can be very large

- the implications of maintaining a component that has been designed for reuse particularly if the reuse is true reuse.

Finally, the initial decision on whether to reuse or to develop should recognise the corporate benefits of reuse as well as the benefits to an individual project. A decision by two projects to share a data structure or one project to reverse engineer a reusable component from another project generates a corporate asset which can be reused by subsequent projects. Deciding when to invest in the development of new reusable components for the future is discussed further in Chapter 8.

7.5 Managing risk

Chapter 4 describes the risks of reuse. This section gives guidance on how these risks can be managed. As a general guideline, risk should be spread; for example, an organisation should not rely on a single supplier to maintain all reusable components.

Maintenance

It is essential that any project which reuses a component is clear how maintenance and support will be performed and by whom. The component may be maintained by either:

- **the component user organisation**. In this case, the organisation must ensure that it has all the resources it needs including expertise in the domain of the component, access to the source code, if necessary, and sufficient understanding of the internal structure of the component. In this case, several of the benefits of reuse are lost

or

- **the supplier**. In this case, the organisation is highly dependent on the supplier. The terms and conditions under which the supplier supports and maintains the component must be clearly understood by both parties.

If the supplier is a commercial one then these terms and conditions should be defined by a contract with penalty clauses. If the supplier is another part of the same organisation, then the terms and conditions should be agreed in writing at a level of management to which both the supplier and the project report.

Writing objective and legally binding terms and conditions for maintenance and support is very difficult. Even then the project must assess the risk of the supplier of the component defaulting or reneging, for example because the supplier company ceases to trade or the library management function is abolished. A last resort approach to this risk is for the project to receive all rights to the component, including its source code and system documentation, by virtue of an ESCROW agreement. A more realistic approach is to use only components from secure and reputable suppliers.

Quality

A component should not be reused until all reasonable investigations have been made into the component's quality. The following questions should be asked:

- does the component and the way it was produced comply with the appropriate quality standards?

- are there reference users of the component who can vouch for its quality?

- has the component been actively maintained by people who fully understand its structure and design?

- does the component have a version history which proves it has been adequately maintained?

If possible, the component should be evaluated on a trial basis, preferably by an expert in the component's domain, before the project commits to using the component.

Legal issues

The way to manage potential legal problems is to recognise their existence (see Chapter 4) and then, if possible, enter into a contractual agreement with the supplier of the component which resolves the issues of ownership and liability in a way which is acceptable to the organisation.

An organisation should take active steps to reduce the extent of ownership problems arising, for example, by ensuring that the organisation owns the Intellectual Property Rights (IPR) of a component developed by a contractor for the organisation.

7.6 The need to change the culture

High levels of reuse require the staff to share. Data management or the management of subroutine libraries are examples of approaches which promote reuse at levels 1 and 2 (see section 3.3). A change of culture is needed to achieve higher levels of reuse; this change must be supported by appropriate organisational structures.

The adoption of the positive approaches described below will help to eliminate many of the barriers to sharing. Nevertheless, senior managers should be alert for indications of problems and barriers to sharing.

7.7 Management support

Management for reuse needs to be plain and clear. It is recommended that the IS strategy is updated to include a section setting out the commitment to reuse and indicating how it is to be achieved in the organisation. Until sharing is firmly established managers need to demonstrate support by frequent words and consistent supportive actions.

7.8 Organisational capability

The organisational capability needed to achieve IS reuse is similar to, and an extension of, that needed for successful data management. Where possible, the new organisational structures should build on the existing data and programme management structures along the lines discussed in Chapters 8, 9 and elsewhere in this volume.

The recognition that many key reuse decisions are made outside individual IS projects is important.

Reuse will not work without the appropriate inter-project roles and responsibilities.

7.9 The Project Initiation Document

The direction of a project is usually set at its inception by the terms of reference set out in the Project Initiation Document (PID). A PID should set out clearly the need for reuse by the project and identify the areas of the project where reuse is expected to be important. The steps in the life-cycle where reuse should be given particular emphasis should be set out. Annex A gives a more detailed analysis of reuse at each SSADM stage. Existing components to be improved and new reusable components to be created by the project should be identified as project deliverables.

Key decisions about what can be reused often need to be made before a development project is started. These decisions are usually made as part of an architecture study, a scoping study, a feasibility study or as a result of work by the data management function. These decisions need to be written into the project's terms of reference so that it is clear to the project what is available and that a budgeted amount of effort should go into reuse. Careful specification in the PID of what is to be reused will avoid many problems later. The project must be planned to allow time to study existing reusable components and to assess how they need to be extended or specialised.

7.10 Providing personal incentives

People often enjoy designing new projects more than extending what already exists. To overcome this, they need to be motivated to exploit opportunities for reuse. Incentives need to be directed away from rewarding quantity, for example, the number of lines of COBOL produced, towards quality, that is very few bugs, fitness for purpose, and the degree of reuse achieved either in terms of existing components or the creation of new reusable components. Prestige is often as important as financial reward. Senior managers should ensure that contributors to the reusable component library are recognised and acknowledged by their managers and peers. Time invested in understanding what is available in the library is time well spent.

Occasional meetings to review the latest additions to the component library are recommended as these give an opportunity for the authors to explain the new functionality of components to their peers.

It may be helpful to discuss staff feelings about *Not Invented Here* at appropriate points in a project that involves reuse, at least in the early days. Meetings should be used to reinforce the benefits of reuse to the project, and to the individual members of the project team.

7.11 Training for Reuse

In order to have the skills to determine what and when to reuse, development staff need:

- cultural training to instil the messages that:

  - reuse is often a better way of building a component than initial development

  - reuse benefits the business and the IT professionals who work in it

  - the IS strategy and the Inter-Project Boards have important roles in providing co-ordination between projects for reuse

- awareness of both personal and business incentives for sharing

- awareness of what is in the library

- knowledge of how to search for and select reusable components using the facilities of the library management system and tools

- the ability to evaluate a reusable component and to compare it with the needs of the IS under development

- improved analysis, design and programming skills to adapt components while maintaining a single source of common functionality.

In addition, there are specialised skills which need to be developed in areas such as library management and how to design and develop reusable components.

7.12 When software development is contracted out

When software development is contracted out, it is still desirable to require the developer to exploit reusable components, and indeed to develop reusable components (see chapter 8), where appropriate.

The Inter-Project Board and individual Project Boards, in such circumstances, are likely to be composed wholly or largely of in-house managers. The Board's requirements of IS development projects to reuse components and create reusable components, as appropriate, remain.

7.13 Measuring reuse

An organisation should measure the degree of reuse which it has achieved. Two specific metrics should be collected:

- The number of times a component in the library has actually been reused. This shows which components are of value to the organisation and, conversely, the components which are not really reusable and do not merit inclusion or retention in the library.

- The proportion of a new information system which is assembled from reusable components. This is a measure of the success of the reuse programme from the IS developer's perspective; it should rise as the organisation gains greater confidence and experience in reuse.

The Component Management Team (see Chapter 9) should be responsible for collecting these metrics and for advising the Inter-Project Board on their interpretation. The Inter-Project Board should continually assess these metrics and take steps which quantitatively improve reuse within the organisation.

8 Building and managing component libraries

We are looking for reuse in at least four areas:

- requirements
- specifications
- designs
- code.

Different types of library are likely to be needed for each category, and probably also for conceptual, external and internal components.

There are potentially three major problems with libraries as discussed in 6.3.

8.1 Managing the library of reusable components

Figure 11 shows one stage of the project life-cycle which highlights the role of the library. The discussion in this chapter is concerned with reusable components which have been produced and are maintained within the organisation. The Inter-Project Board is not responsible for reusable components which are supplied and maintained by a third party.

The Inter-Project Board must decide how active or passive the library management function should be. An active service takes much of the responsibility for the reusable components which it manages. With a more passive free-market approach, library management has less responsibility for:

- evaluating and certifying reusable components
- fixing faults
- maintaining a coherent library structure.

The active service requires more investment that is not directly tied to a project than the passive service. For this reason, it is likely that library management in many organisations will be passive in the short term.

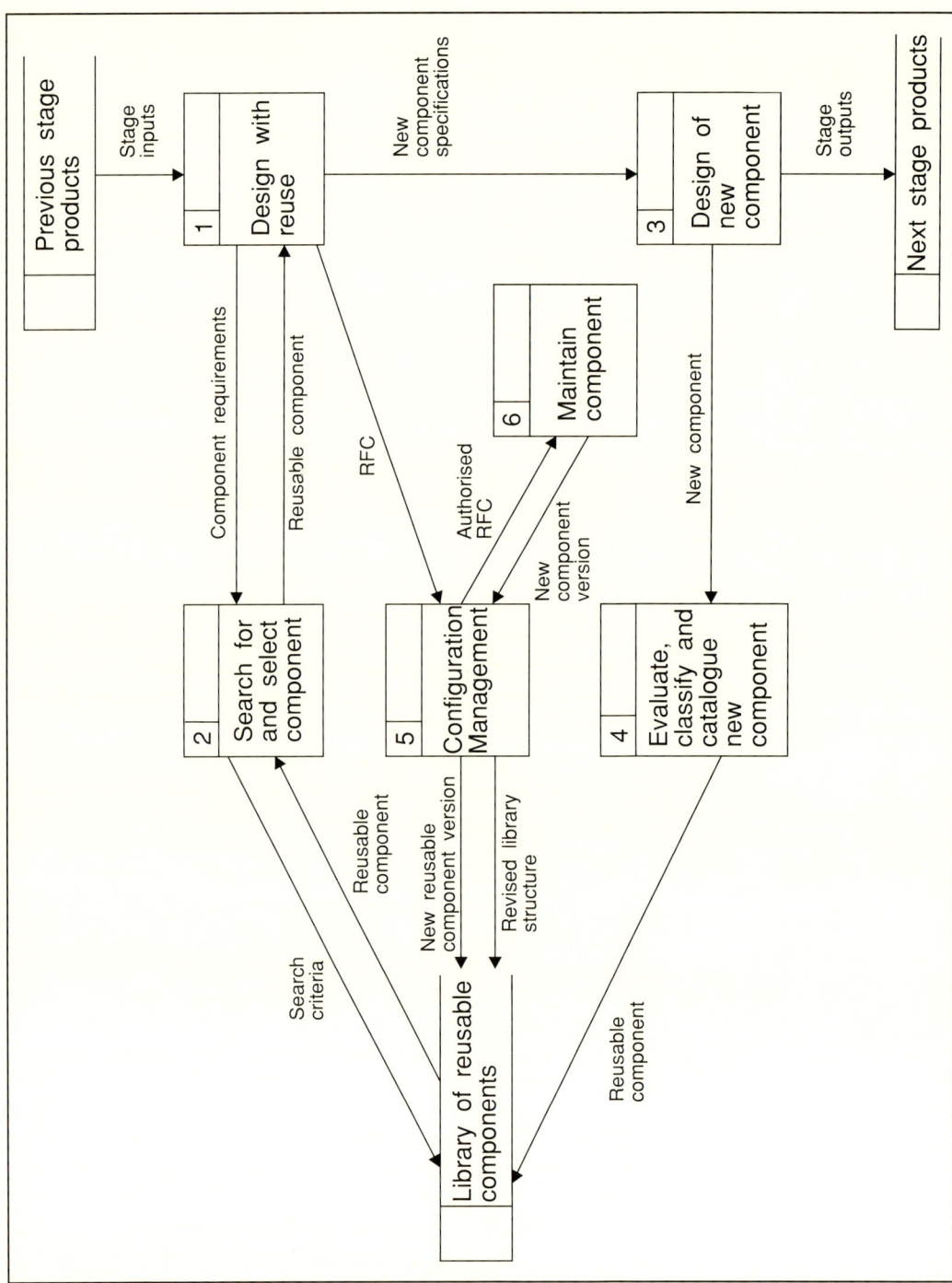

Figure 11: Component management dataflows

Longer term, library management will be more active as the benefits of reuse are realised.

The following sections describe the principal activities involved in library management:

- providing facilities for users of the library to search for reusable components which meet their needs

- adding a new component to the library if it is useful, maintainable and of adequate quality

- managing changes to components held in the library

- ensuring the security and integrity of the library.

8.2 Searching for reusable components

There is potential to reuse components at every stage of the IS life-cycle. Library management must allow the library to be searched efficiently and effectively for components which match these requirements. Users of the library must be offered reusable components which closely match their requirements as well as those which exactly match their requirements. Users then have the option of adapting the component to meet their particular requirements.

Library management tools can be very effective in providing services such as:

- browsing the library and navigating from one component to a related component

- searching for reusable components on the basis of keywords.

Users should be provided with the candidate component and information about it, in particular:

- full documentation for the component

- any known faults or limitations in the component

- the derivation of the component, that is, its version history, how frequently and where it has been used.

8.3 Adding a new component to the library

When a component has been designed for reuse or when considering an existing component for addition the following criteria need to be considered:

- is it general purpose or is its utility limited to a particular application?

- does it comply with the organisation's standards and policies, including quality requirements, for IS?

- is the component adequately documented for users other than its designers?

- what is the level of confidence that the component complies with its documentation. For example, what level of testing and use has it received?

- will it be maintained by its provider? If not, does the Inter-Project Board command the resources needed to maintain the component?

A more detailed discussion of what makes a component reusable follows later in this chapter. If the component passes this evaluation it is certified, classified and added to the library.

8.4 Configuration management

The evolution of reusable components in the library must be subject to configuration management. The Component Management Team must write a configuration management plan which must be approved by the Inter-Project Board (see *PRINCE: Reference Manual* for details).

Change control

The Inter-Project Board serves as the Change Control Board for the component library. It is responsible for ensuring that each Request For Change (RFC) to a library component is evaluated, authorised or rejected, and if it is authorised, then implemented and approved. The Inter-Project Board must ensure that the views of all users of the component are represented in evaluating the importance of the RFC.

The change control function is particularly important if all the users of a reusable component must use the same version of the component. For example, the projects of the Inland Revenue Corporation Tax Pay and File programme (see Chapter 3) must each use the same version of each CLUMP because the CLUMP defines the structure of shared data. In this case, the Inter-Project Board must co-ordinate the adoption of a new version of the reusable component by the projects which use it.

Version control

A project using a reusable component from the library may tailor that component to improve its utility in the project context. Such changes may be to extend, correct or adapt the component.

The project may propose to the Inter-Project Board that the new version of the component is an improvement on the original and that the new version should be entered into the library. The Inter-Project Board has the following options to consider:

- hold both versions of the reusable component in the library and allow library users to decide which to reuse

- evaluate the two versions and determine that one is an improvement over the other

- merge the best parts of the two versions to create a third version which supersedes the other two.

The third of the three options is the best from the viewpoint of library users, but it is also the most demanding. Although software tools can be of great assistance in the merge process, a good understanding of the component's structure and design is also required.

Tools	The library of reusable components should be held in electronic form. Components should be transferred between the library and projects in electronic form. Practical experience has shown that a paper based component library is difficult and expensive to manage and is under used.
	A software tool for managing components must support all configuration management functions and preserve the structure of the components it holds. For example, the library should not hold a logical data model as a bit-map picture and unstructured text but as properly structured entities and relationships which are described by individual data dictionary entries.
	In the long term, standards such as IRDS may provide this structure (see Chapter 6). In the short term, the Component Management Team should adopt the best practice described in section 6.3, that is use proprietary repositories and pragmatic methods and tools to migrate components between repositories and CASE tools. The Component Management Team must recognise that configuration management is even more important in such a heterogeneous environment.
Security	The library of reusable components contains the software assets of an organisation. From the perspective of risk management, these assets are all concentrated in one place. The library must, therefore, be secure from unauthorised access. Both read and write access must be controlled, the former to prevent unauthorised disclosure and the latter to prevent unauthorised change or deletion. Insecure access to the library can arise from accidental or malicious corruption and from well-intentioned but misguided attempts to by-pass controls.
	Fraudulent access is an important issue if reusable components manage financial assets, for example bank accounts or tax returns. In this case the library must be secure against unauthorised updates. Some library management tools and operating systems provide mandatory and discretionary access controls (see *DoD 5200.28-STD, Department of Defence Trusted Computer System Evaluation Criteria*). Another approach

Chapter 8
Building and managing component libraries

is for an independent authority to audit every change to the library.

Prevention of unauthorised access is also important if the library service is funded by designers who should pay to use a library component. It is, however, extremely difficult to prevent the unauthorised copying of a reusable component once it has been checked out of the library as most copy protection facilities can be circumvented.

8.5 When to invest in new reusable components

Previous chapters of this volume have concentrated on the consumer's perspective of whether, when and how to reuse an existing component. The remainder of this chapter considers when and how a reusable component should be produced within an organisation.

This section discusses when it is appropriate to invest in the development of a reusable component. Section 8.6 describes the functional attributes of a good reusable component. Section 8.7 describes the quality attributes.

In general reusable components should be built when the following conditions apply:

- the components required by the organization do not already exist and are not available from their organizations

- a market, internally or externally, exists for the reusable component

- the organization has the skills and the will to develop and market the components

- the business case for doing so, taking a sufficiently long view, is positive.

Building larger, more strategic components

Decisions concerning when to build larger, more strategic reusable components should be taken by the Inter-Project Board during the development of the programme plan.

The Project Board of the project that will build such a reusable component will ratify the decision during the early stages of a project. That decision will be reviewed by the project team during an SSADM Feasibility Study at step 030 and during Requirements Analysis at steps 210 and 220 (Business Systems Options), see Annex A. The degree to which a project will evaluate whether or not to build a reusable quality component should be set down in the PID following the direction of the Inter-Project Board. In some cases, the whole purpose of the project will be to build the reusable component.

If the project decides it should not build a reusable component that the Inter-Project Board directed that it should build, the matter must be referred back to the Inter-Project Board for resolution before the project is allowed to proceed.

Building smaller reusable components	It is likely that smaller components will not be explicitly planned for and built. Rather, they will be offered by enthusiastic project team members as contributions to the library. The Component Management Team will then assess the offering and, if suitable, make it available more widely.
Building reusable components costs more	Realistically, a component which is planned to be reused must be designed to have a higher quality than one which will remain confined within one project. The documentation must be top quality. The analysis and design will be exposed to the criticisms of others. More bugs will be found as the software is used in ways not envisaged by the designers. Thus, more effort must be planned for the analysis, design, construction, testing and maintenance of a reusable component.

In addition, a reusable component will often be designed so that it has complete or well rounded functionality to encourage its reuse. During analysis, the requirements of a range of customers may be assessed. Conversely, a component designed for a single project will have as little functionality as possible.

Making a commercial decision	The additional cost of building a marketable reusable component, of making it available and keeping it available, must be assessed. Even if the intended scope of reuse is only within the originating organisation, there will still be some marketing, possibly informal, and also support and maintenance activity.
	The size of the market for the reusable component must be determined. This may be only two or three projects within the organisation. Alternatively there may be an external market. If the software is to be made available outside the originating organisation, there will be legal costs and product liability issues to consider.
	The savings and revenue arising from the creation of the reusable component should be assessed and compared with the cost of development to determine whether an adequate return on investment is likely.
Taking a view across the whole organisation	The development of a high quality reusable component within a project that will only use it once is unlikely to be cost justified. However, there may be a considerable cost justification if the component is to be used several times by a number of projects.
	The project developing the reusable component will have to be funded to produce a high quality component in the knowledge that the savings will come as the component is used in other projects. The Inter-Project Board will make the decision on whether or not to allocate the necessary funds.
Ensuring the additional funds are well spent	The PID must set out the quality criteria for the component to ensure that the additional funds do yield a marketable component. The Project Board is responsible for supplying the reusable component to the Inter-Project Board.

8.6 Functional attributes

In terms of their functional attributes reusable components should be both general and complete.

General
A reusable component is one which can be reused in many different contexts and, therefore, it must be general purpose. For example, a stack of items of arbitrary type is more reusable than a stack of integers.

There are risks, however, in making a component too general purpose as the:

- component may become complex and difficult to use
- domain specific properties of the component may be lost
- component may become large and unwieldy.

Complete
The amount of functionality a component should have requires careful judgement. For example, a stack component without a pop operation is clearly incomplete, but should the stack operation also provide a way of determining the depth of the stack?

Functionality for a project specific component should only be provided if it is needed. Functionality for a reusable component should be provided if it is likely to be needed and the business case for providing it is positive.

However, there are similar risks in providing completeness in a reusable component as there are in providing generality. The designer of the reusable component must balance the opposing arguments.

8.7 Quality attributes

The quality attributes of reusable components are such that the components should be:

- Robust
- Maintainable
- Documented
- Loosely coupled and highly cohesive
- Portable.

Robust	The user of a reusable component will expect the component to work reliably. The user will not expect to test the component, submit fault reports to the component's supplier nor necessarily to correct the faults. A component must therefore be rigorously tested, verified and validated before it is offered for reuse.
Maintainable	A useful reusable component will have a long life during which it is likely to be extensively adapted, corrected and extended. The component may be maintained by its supplier, by its user or as a library management function. Whoever maintains the component, it is important that: • it is well structured • the quality of the component does not degrade with extensive maintenance • the implementation of the component is documented so that it can be maintained by staff other than its developers.
Documented	To select a component, a potential user must know: • its functional behaviour • its performance • what it depends upon. A component will not be selected from the library if it is not clear what the component does and how it does it. A reusable component must therefore be documented carefully and precisely. Formal notations (such as Z and VDM) are the most reliable means of specifying a reusable component precisely because of the ambiguities inherent in English. Unfortunately these notations require skills of writers and readers which are not yet widespread.

| Loosely coupled and highly cohesive | Like any well designed component, a reusable component should exhibit weak coupling with other components. |

The component should be loosely coupled to:

- components which use it, that is, the interface between the component and its users should be as simple as possible. There is a potential conflict here with the need for generality which leads to a complex interface. The designer of a reusable component must balance this conflict and recognise that a component with a complex interface is hard to reuse

- other components. The danger in using a particular component is that a developer acquires many other components upon which the reusable component depends, its baggage, and which require machine resources such as memory.

A corollary of loose coupling between components is that components should be highly cohesive. Each reusable component should have a single well-defined purpose which relates all its constituent elements and there should be no redundant elements in the component.

| Portable | A component which is portable between several environments and platforms, for example VME, Unix, MS-DOS..., has much more potential for reuse than one which can only be used in one environment. Compliance with standards for languages and data structures (see Chapter 6) is a valuable policy for achieving portability. |

9 Inter-project roles and responsibilities

Reuse at levels 1 and 2 can be achieved by a single project without support and management from outside the project. To achieve reuse at levels 3 and 4, new roles and responsibilities are needed which co-ordinate reuse between projects. This chapter describes these roles and responsibilities.

9.1 Management direction and technical work

As described in Chapter 3, reuse applies to business procedures, analysis and design as well as program code. The earlier that opportunities for reuse are identified in the life-cycle, the larger are the benefits.

Early identification of major reuse opportunities should come from strategy studies, scoping studies and ongoing data management work.

Reuse between projects needs to be co-ordinated by a role termed in this volume the Inter-Project Board. This board needs to be supported by an executive function which is likely to evolve out of an existing Data Management Group. In this volume, this technical function is termed the Component Management Team. If there is already a Data Management Group then its responsibilities should be extended to include the responsibilities of the Component Management Team.

Where there is already an IS development Programme Board or an IS Planning Secretariat, then these roles, preferably the first, should be extended to cover the responsibilities of the Inter-Project Board. If business-change programmes are responsible for their own IS development projects, and there is no overall IS development programme, then the Inter-Project Board will have to coordinate reuse among projects that straddle several programmes.

9.2 Inter-Project Boards

Each Inter-Project Board:

- has a broad but shallow view of the projects it co-ordinates

- is responsible for the overall structure, in relation to data and processing, of the systems it manages

- determines, after taking appropriate technical advice, which components should be reused by its projects

- encourages its project boards to make use of existing reusable components and, wherever it can, specifies which these shall be

- encourages its project boards to produce reusable components and, wherever it can, specifies which these shall be

- encourages its project boards to adopt open technologies

- is responsible for the admission of reusable components to the library and the overall management of the library and its components

- assigns, after taking appropriate technical advice, the responsibility for the maintenance of each reusable component

- authorises the definition (name, classification, description) of each reusable component; rules in favour of one of the contending definitions when there is disagreement.

The Inter-Project Board is responsible for strategic aspects of how systems are developed. This is both a business and a technical role. Issues concerning the introduction of common procedures throughout an organisation and the sharing of data are crucial business decisions. The balancing of short term needs and longer term savings is an important aspect of when to reuse. Such decisions must be made at the business level.

9.3 The Component Management Team

Reuse requires the existence of a function independent of the project teams to maintain, develop and promote the library of common components which encapsulate business or technical knowledge. In an organisation committed to data management, this should be a natural extension of the role of the Data Management Team. They start to manage common functionality as well as data. Senior Management should plan for the Data Management Team to evolve into the Component Management Team over three to four years.

An organisation that has no data management function should establish one as a first step towards greater reuse.

It is important to recognise that the Component Management Team plays a pro-active role. They seek out commonality of function and data. They act as the executive arm of the Inter-Project Board but they are much more than a mere library function. The Component Management Team should contain experienced designers and staff with a broad knowledge of the organisation's business.

The Component Management Team has responsibilities for:

- providing technical support to the Inter-Project Board

- acting as secretariat and executive arm to the Inter-Project Board

- designing the overall systems structure, including the data model

- deciding which business functions are to have their IS provided by means of shared IS components, after discussion with appropriate managers

- deciding which data will be shared across the whole business after discussion with the appropriate managers

- managing the library of reusable components

- collecting the reuse metrics.

A senior member of the Component Management Team should belong to the Inter-Project Board.

9.4 Organisational relationships

Figure 12 gives an overview of the organisational relationships.

The Inter-Project Board is concerned with translating the strategy into plans for programmes or a portfolio of individual projects.

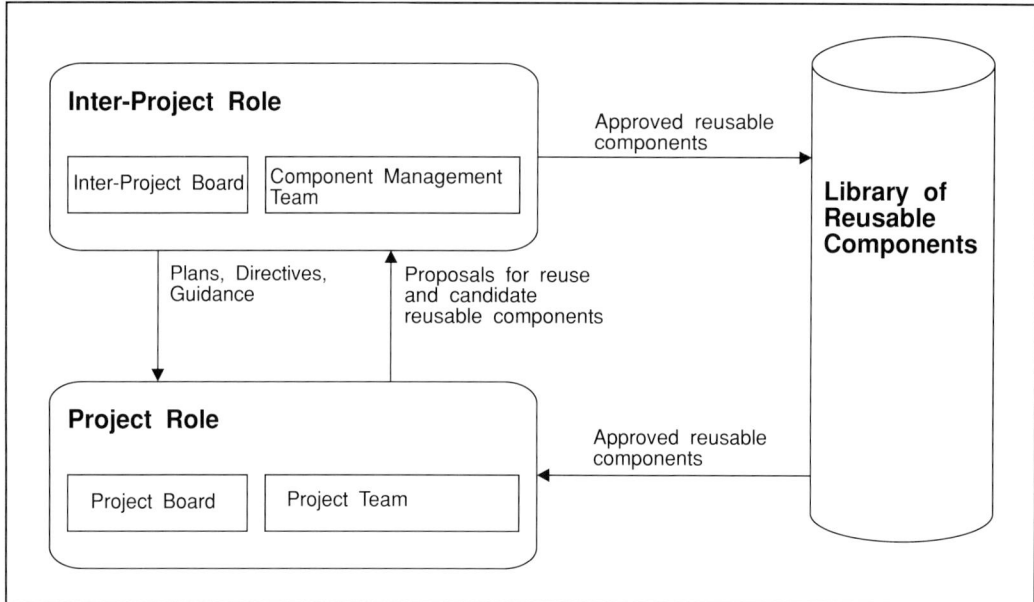

Figure 12: Overview of organisational relationships to support reuse

The Inter-Project Board and the Component Management Team are responsible for the coordination of projects and the maintenance of the library of reusable components.

There may be a need for more than one level of co-ordination in an organisation of considerable size. In this case, each Inter-Project Board would manage several projects within the same programme. This is explored in the examples in section A.5.

Figure 13 shows a more detailed view of the flows identified in figure 12 above.

Chapter 9
Inter-project roles and responsibilities

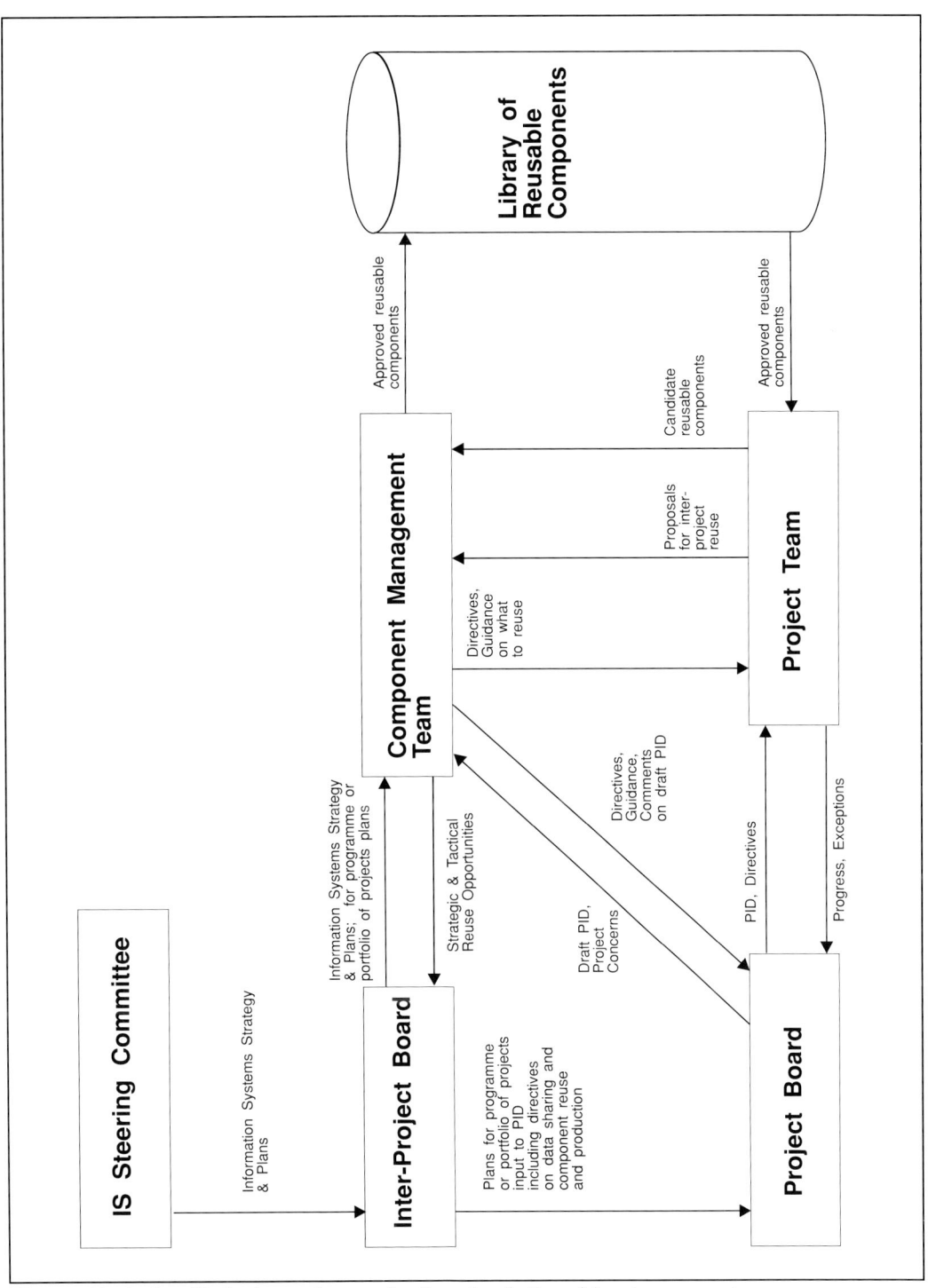

Figure 13: A detailed view of organisational relationships to support reuse

9.5 Examples of organisational structures to support reuse

This section outlines a number of alternative organisational approaches adopted to promote reuse in organisations of varying size. Experience of these organisations has been used as the basis for organisational recommendations in this volume.

Ordnance Survey

In Ordnance Survey, there are Project Boards for the Corporate Data Management team and for the Topological Data Management System (TDMS) team. The Corporate Data Management team takes a view across all applications. The TDMS team is primarily responsible for technical (topographic) data architecture, that is managing a programme of related projects. The work of these two architectural teams is closely co-ordinated with a good working relationship between them. The Project Boards have some commonality of membership. New applications concerned with the delivery of map data to customers are requiring an increasing degree of integration and data sharing between application areas that had hitherto been stand alone.

Inland Revenue

The Inland Revenue has an architecture team responsible for the data and application architecture of a programme to re-engineer the Corporation Tax Pay and File system. This team is the guardian of the CLUMPS (see section 3.4). The team give technical direction to the project teams within the programme.

The IBM software library

The IBM software library has been set up for IBM systems programmers. Proposed components are assessed for quality, rated and certified by a central library management function. There are financial incentives for populating the library and the incentives are greater if the quality of the component is judged to be high. Individual projects are encouraged to use components in the library. No other management structure is required in this case.

The National Health Service

The NHS is a very distributed organisation. The NHS Management Centre (see Chapter 3) is a central function that funds projects in specific hospitals or

Chapter 9
Inter-project roles and responsibilities

districts to develop components to a quality of documentation that is reusable throughout the NHS.

Ministry of Defence

More than one level of coordination may be needed in a large organisation. Figure 14 shows the Ministry of Defence (MOD) multi-level organisation of Data Management Groups. There is one team at the centre. There is a Data Management group per Function. There are a number of Functional Areas within each Function, each of which can have many projects. Opportunities for reuse are primarily within Function.

There is a permanent team and a management committee at each level. Each management committee takes formal decisions concerning shared data and gives direction to the management committee's Data Management Group.

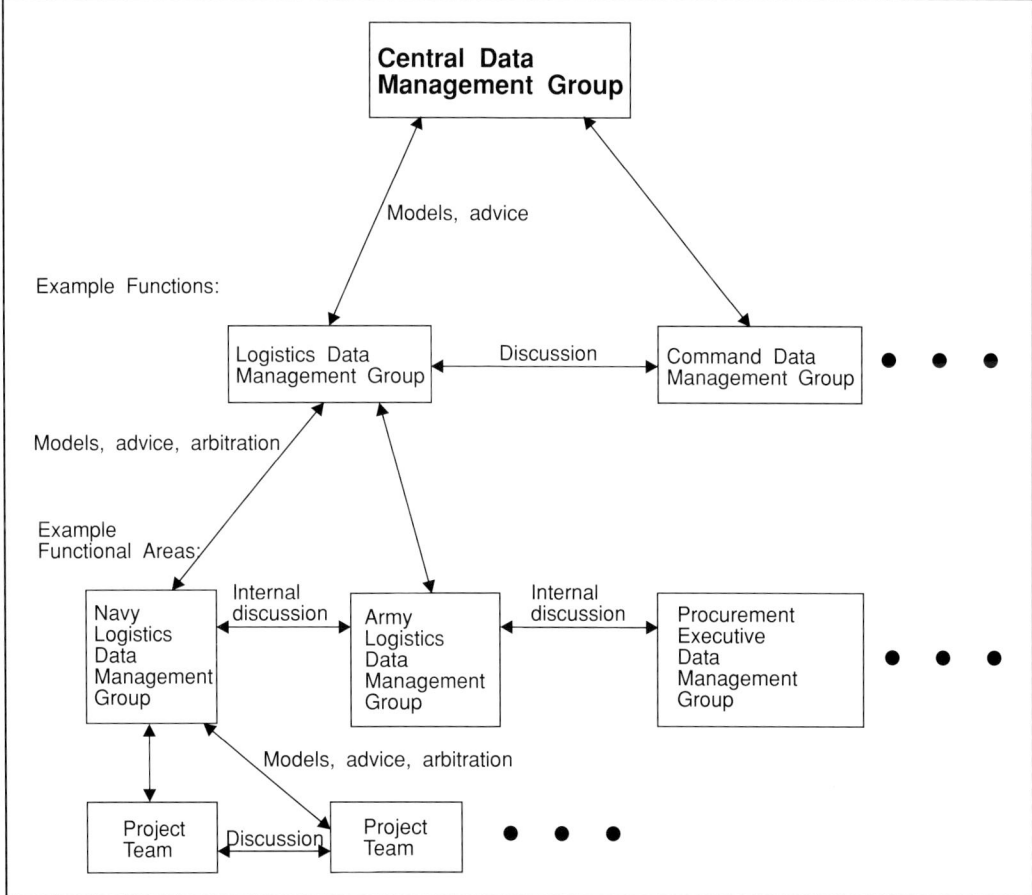

Figure 14: MOD organisation to support reuse through data management

A Tailoring SSADM for reuse

A.1 Tailoring SSADM techniques

Section 5.5 outlined some areas where reuse can be achieved without extending the current SSADM method. What is needed is a central function and library, communication, management and culture as described elsewhere.

The world seems to be slowly moving towards a much more object-oriented approach to systems. SSADM is quite object-oriented, for example entity life histories, which model the behaviour of entities, have been part of SSADM for a long time. Do not wait for SSADM to become more object-oriented to achieve reuse. By setting up an effective Data Management function and evolving it into a full Component Management function which handles process sharing as well as data sharing, an organisation can achieve significant benefits now.

The following subsections point to areas of current SSADM that are particularly important for reuse.

Sub-typing

The *SSADM Version 4 Reference Manual* defines a way of documenting general entity types, termed super-types, and the more specific sub-types. The manual states that the super-type has attributes and relationships which are common to its sub-types. Sub-types may be overlapping. Thus, a basic type *Person* may usefully be categorised into sub-types *Male* and *Female*. Additional to this there may also be an important partition according to whether a person is an *Employee* or a *Pensioner*. This leads to the further sub-types *Employed Males*, *Retired Males*, *Employed Females* and *Retired Females*.

The identification of such type hierarchies is particularly important in seeking opportunities for reuse. Another project may have specified processing for a very similar sub-type. Identification of the common super-type and consideration of what processing applies to both sub-types is a key step.

Thus, when considering reuse, the analyst should seek to identify similar types and to determine the

	super-types. In addition to determining common attributes and relationships, the analyst should look for commonality of entity identifiers, constraints and aspects of life histories.
Entity Life Histories	Entity life histories for the sub-types and super-types should be created independently and then compared intuitively. This will give an understanding of the commonality of processing across different sub-types and hence indicate what can be reused.
	Note the use of the word *intuitively*. At present there is no widely agreed technique for determining the inheritance of all or parts of a life history by a sub-type. This is an area of academic research and its introduction into SSADM is likely to be some way off.
Data Flow Diagrams	The use of the Data Flow Modelling technique can be extended so that context diagrams are produced that show the data flows between several systems. These very high level context diagrams can then be used to identify application sized reusable components.
Processes	There are no strong principles for matching processes which is therefore harder than matching entities. This should not however prevent the consideration of existing processes or the design of processes for reuse.

A.2 Tailoring activities and information flows

The example which follows shows one way of tailoring SSADM

The revised structural model diagrams	Figure A.1 shows that the Project Team interacts with the Component Management Team and uses the library of shared components throughout the life-cycle.
	Figure A.1 shows the role of the Component Management Team as collectors of reusable components which are placed in the shared library. The figure shows that there is a formal input by the Component Management Team at the beginning of each SSADM stage. The project's products are stored

in the library as potential reusable components at the end of each stage. The components that have been specifically engineered for reusability are marked.

A more detailed view showing the flows to and from particular steps is given in Figures A.2 to A.6. See the following sections.

The key additions, in respect of reuse, to all of these figures are the flows into and out of the Component Management Team. They are shown in larger, italicised type for emphasis.

Certain flows are labelled as discussion flows rather than as product flows. The intent is to encourage person to person interaction at these key points.

Information Systems Engineering Library
Managing Reuse

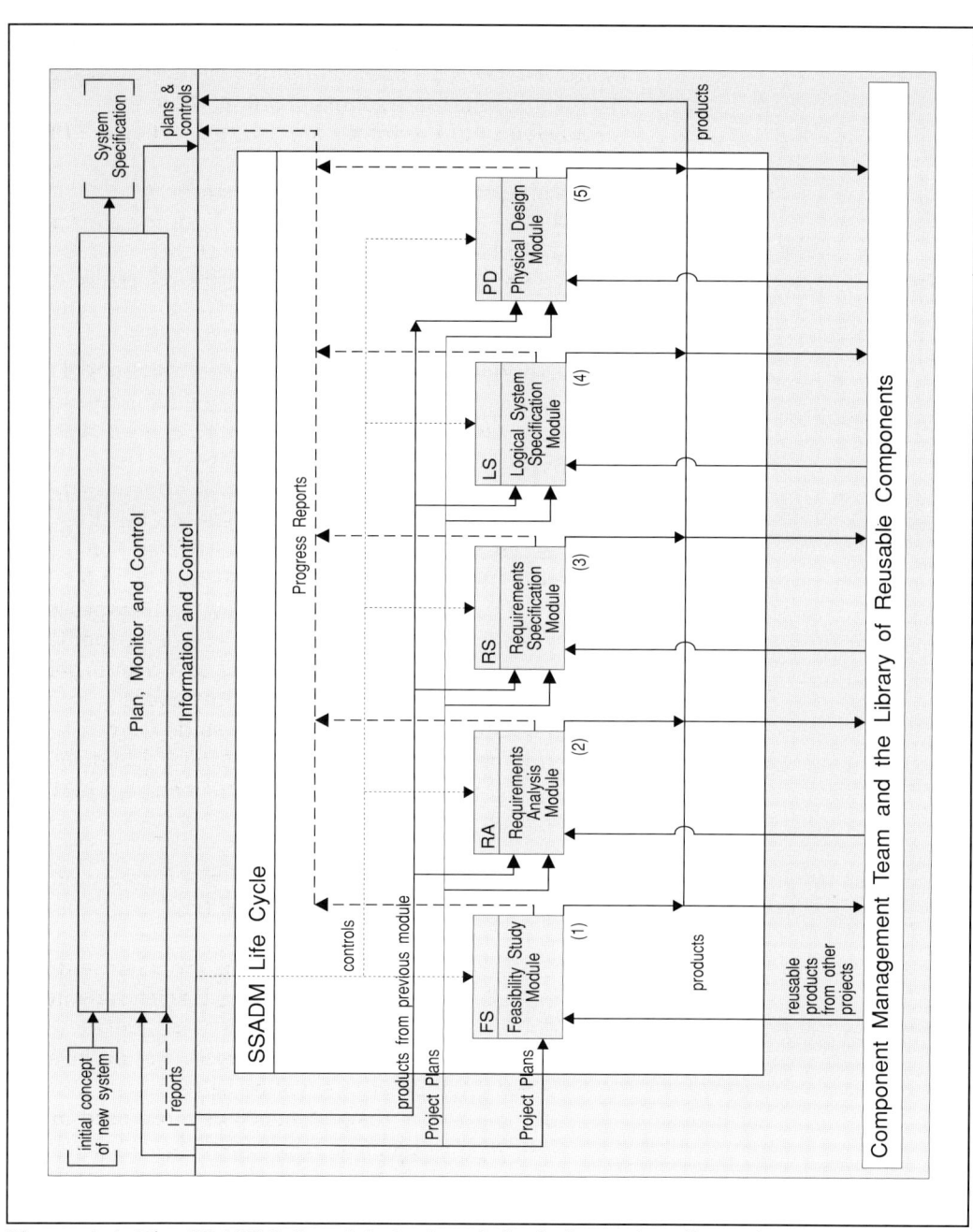

Figure A.1: The SSADM Core Method and the information flows for reuse

New types of product

A number of new types of product are shown in the figures A.1 to A.5. These are products of the work of the Component Management Team and are the responsibility of the Inter-Project Board. They are the:

- **Infrastructure System Architecture**. A specification of the scope of each of the current and planned systems, in terms of their responsibilities for entities and the interfaces between these systems.

- **Corporate Data Model**. A logical data model, diagrams and all associated entity, relationships and attribute definitions, covering all current and planned systems, or the systems that it is practical to cover, and also showing how systems share data. The behaviour of entities must be understood in order to facilitate reuse. For example, two order entity definitions may be quite different when their entity life histories are considered, but similar when seen only from the point of view of their attributes and relationships. Thus, documentation of the entity event modelling as well as the more static view provided by the entity, relationship and attribute documentation should be maintained as a part of the Corporate Data Model

- **Data Sharing Architecture**. A specification of which systems share which entities

- **Corporate Process Model**. This model should include a top level Data Flow Diagram showing flows between systems. When an overall understanding is being developed, a multi-level view of the processes will be helpful; decomposition diagrams such as those used in Information Engineering or the Oracle CASE Method should be used to document the identity and status of reusable components

- **Policy for Physical Data Sharing**. A specification of how data sharing is reflected in physical database design, at the level of which tables are in which databases and used by which systems. In complex cases, this will need to include details of which parts of an entity's life history are managed by which systems and the period for which knowledge of the entity resides in a particular database.

The SSADM core method and the information flows	Neither the project team nor the Component Management Team is able to predict all useful reuse of a project's work. All formal products should be fed back for reuse at the end of each Module and held on a project products section of the library. However, they should be carefully marked so that it is clear which products are explicitly intended for reuse and have been checked for consistency with corporate data and functional models and/or the corporate database design/function architecture. Those items that are project specific or which have not been rigorously quality checked should be marked so that their status as project products is clear. The complete configuration management facilities of the library should be used.
	There should be informal communication between the project and the Component Management Team during each stage. In particular, the Component Management Team compares project data and process models with the organisation's overall data and process models for the business area in question. The project works with the Component Management Team to ensure that its extensions to the overall data and process models are consistent with the developing corporate models. Similarly, the database structures should be developed in a way that is consistent with other projects sharing the same database during physical design. The transaction design should be developed so that it is consistent with the physical design of other systems.
	The following subsections look at the information flows during each of the SSADM stages and give an overview of the activities to promote reuse.
Feasibility study module	At the beginning of the Feasibility Study, the project team should collect all existing information (see figure A.2) concerning the current system and the other data models that have common entity types. The

Component Management Team advises the project team of what is relevant. This information will include the corporate products described above and existing SSADM documentation for the current system and those systems that interface, or could interface, to the proposed system.

The system architecture enables the project team to position the proposed system precisely and to be aware of all the necessary interfaces. It defines which system is the master system for each entity and which system has update responsibility.

The corporate data model is the basis for identification of entity types that are common to the proposed system and other systems. It is considerably easier to spot common entity types than to spot common processes. Common entity types naturally bring along their entity life histories and associated processes. Thus, this data-oriented approach is emphasised in this volume as a matter of practicality. However, all SSADM products, not just data-oriented products, are capable of reuse.

The scope of the project is defined in terms of the part of the overall data model it addresses. The Component Management Team reviews the scope with the project team to identify opportunities for sharing and reuse not considered by the Project Identification Document.

The corporate process model provides the data flow framework into which the proposed system fits.

Use of the current system documentation saves considerable re-analysis.

As the project team undertake step 020, Define the Problem, they may develop a Logical Data Model and Data Flow Model or improve existing models. This should be done working with the Component Management Team to ensure that the project's view is properly integrated with the Corporate models.

During the analysis of the options, the project team discusses the degree to which each of the Feasibility Options supports the IS strategy, the data and system architectures and the planned degree of reuse and data sharing with the Component Management Team. The Feasibility Report is retained in the Library.

At the end of the Feasibility Study, some projects will have done substantial analysis which can be fed back to the Component Management Team. Other projects may do very little detailed work during this stage. Where substantial work has been done, the new or revised Logical Data Model for the product and any extensions to the entity event modelling will be merged back into the overall Corporate Model by the Component Management Team and the project working together. New processes and flows identified by the project team will be integrated into the overall process model.

This integration exercise will clearly define the interfaces that the proposed system will have with other systems and will identify any necessary changes to those systems at a high level. While the Project Board is responsible for its own project, the Inter Project Board is responsible for ensuring that the work to implement any changes to the systems is planned.

Annex A
Tailoring SSADM for reuse

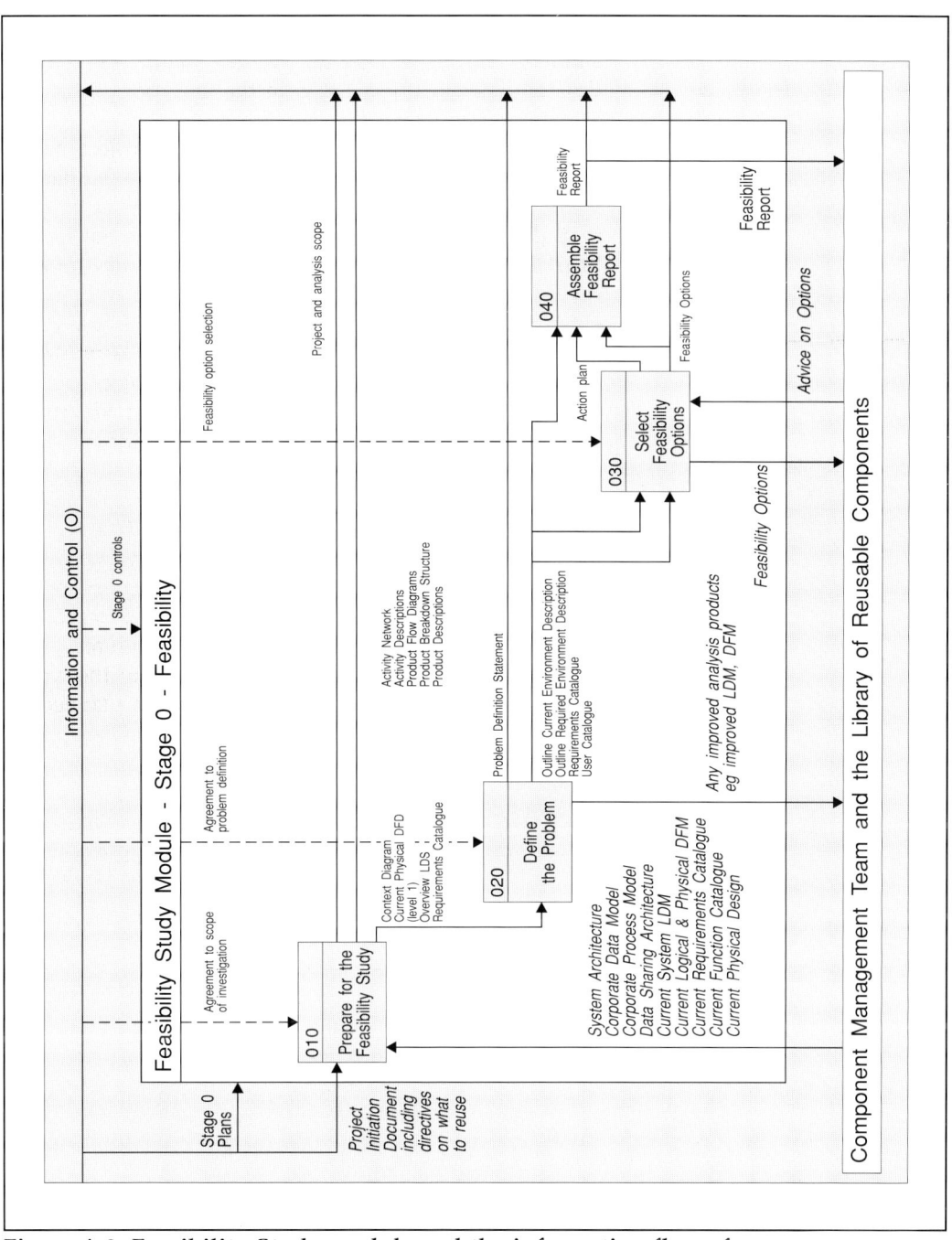

Figure A.2: Feasibility Study module and the information flows for reuse

Requirements Analysis Module	The information flows during the Requirements Analysis Module (see figure A.3) are similar to those during the Feasibility Study. However, more detailed information is required by the project team and, in return, they supply more detailed models. The way in which the project team and the CMT liaise is similar. During this stage a first identification of functions and data that already exist and are candidates for reuse is made.

Existing entity specifications should be reused or enhanced if the required entities already exist in the corporate data model. Even if an exact match is not apparent, attention should be given to matching sub-types and super-types of entities in the corporate data model.

Identical kinds of events should be identified and traced through to effects and entities in the corporate data model. Those functions that have been defined to handle single events are strong candidates for matching and reuse. However, the matching process should work from entity types, events and effects rather than from function definitions. This is because SSADM function definitions are an arbitrary grouping of effects.

Requirements catalogue and user catalogue entries are not as formally defined as the data modelling concepts and are therefore less reusable. They should be treated by the analysts as useful background information.

The products assembled during step 160 are passed to the Component Management Team and held on the library.

During the analysis of the Business Systems Options, the project team discusses the degree to which each of the Business Systems Options supports the Information Systems Strategy, the data and system architectures and the planned degree of reuse and data sharing with the Component Management Team.

Annex A
Tailoring SSADM for reuse

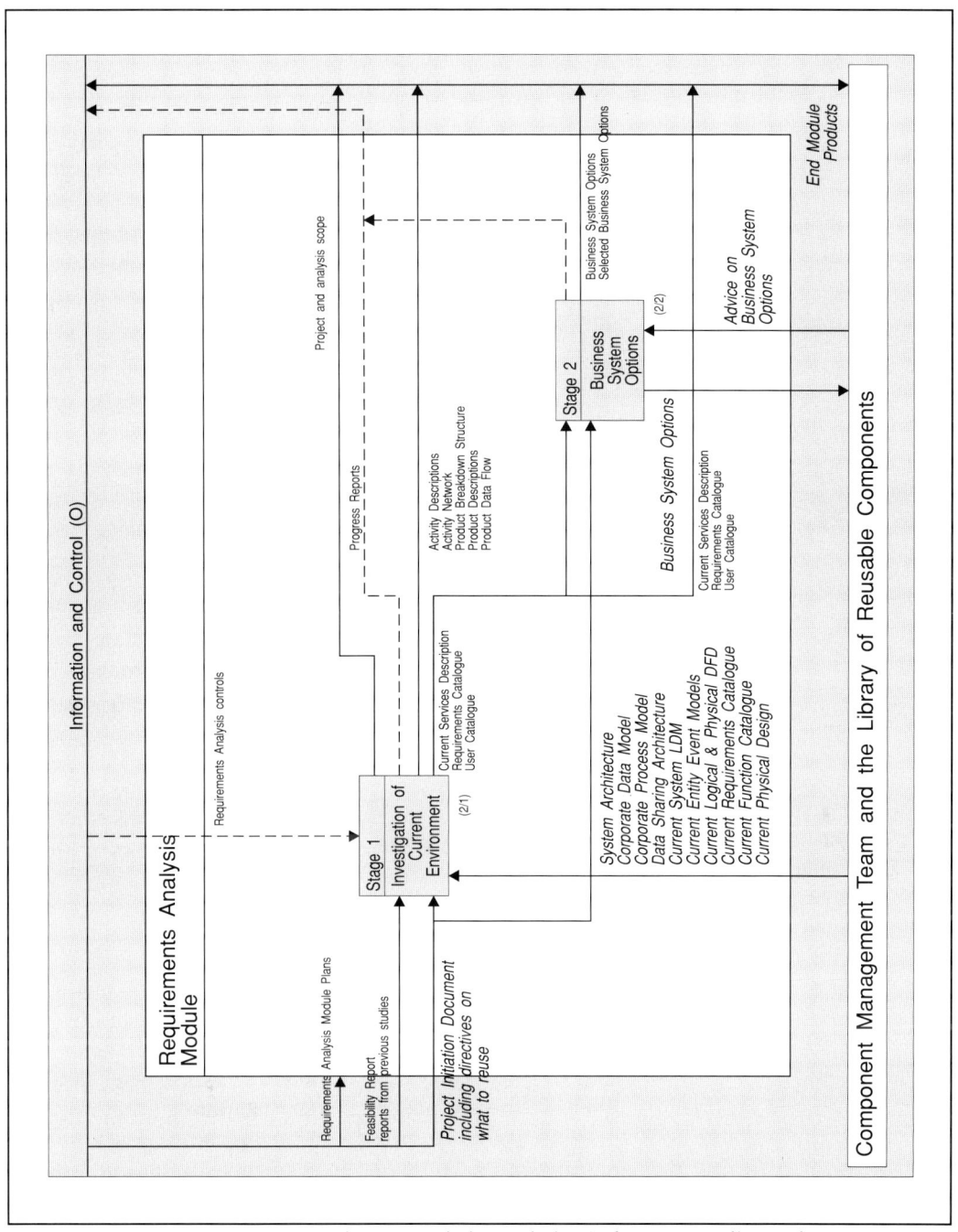

Figure A.3: Requirements Analysis module and the information flows for reuse

Evaluation work done to assess the different options during step 210 should be retained in the library for use by other projects addressing similar issues. For example, where a project has evaluated whether to build a Windows-based Human Computer Interface, the arguments used could be relevant to many projects. However, the nature of the material that can be reused is likely to vary widely in scope and usefulness. Identification of such material relies on the skills of the Component Management Team rather than on a particular process.

Requirements Specification module

During Requirements Specification, there is detailed interaction between the project team and the Component Management Team to agree reusable data definitions and process definitions. Input to step 310 includes the System Architecture, the Corporate Data Model, the Corporate Process Model, the Data Sharing Architecture and details of existing data flow and process models. Some of these define the interfaces for the new system. Others are potentially reusable processing components. Input to step 320 includes the corporate data model, the data sharing architecture and the policy for physical data sharing.

Figure A.4 shows the most important informal interactions at steps 340 and 360 but there are other interactions throughout the Requirements Specification Stage.

During step 340, the project proposes extensions to the corporate data model and agrees these with the Component Management Team. Where the system uses entities whose master update is carried out by another system, the Component Management Team will ensure that the project share data and does not build its own conflicting update system.

During step 360, the project proposes extensions to the corporate process model and agrees these with the Component Management Team. The analyst should search for processes in the required system that have identical or similar data flows triggered by the same events to other processes in the corporate process model. Processes are likely to be similar if their access to entities is similar. The analyst can consider whether the flows between process and end user are similar enough to be able to reuse some or all of a process specification.

At the end of step 380, the Requirements Specification is passed to the Component Management Team for holding in the library.

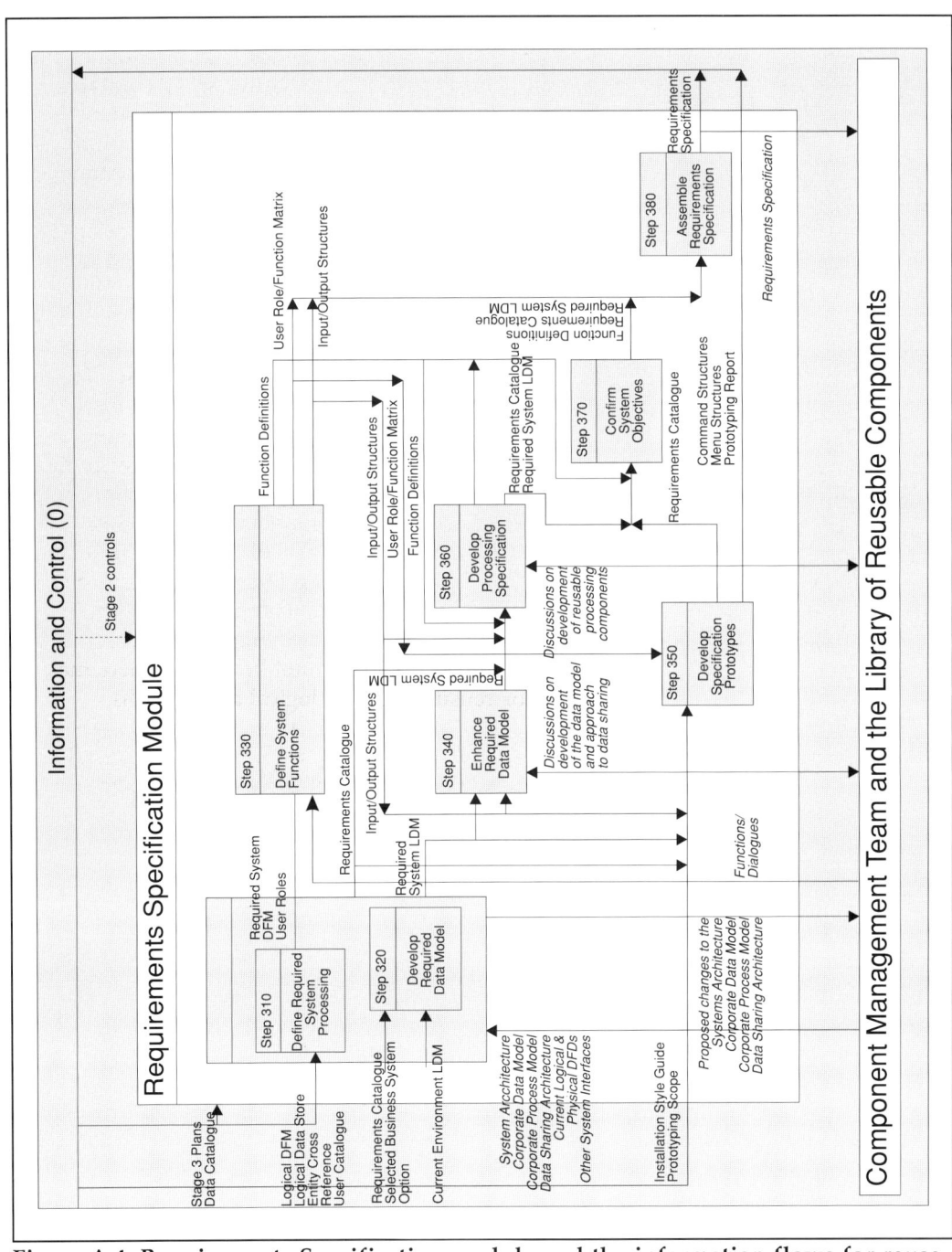

Figure A.4: Requirements Specification module and the information flows for reuse

Logical System Specification module	During Stage 4, Technical System Options (see figure A.5), the Component Management Team specifies the approach for physical data sharing and the database design options during step 410. The Component Management Team work with the project team to ensure that the approach to the data sharing strategy can be achieved within the constraints of the project during step 420. Any failure to achieve the desired level of integration towards the end of Stage 4 is referred to the Inter-Project Board.
	Stage 5, Logical Design, is the key point for confirmation of processes that can be re-used. The Component Management Team supply potentially reusable update process models at the beginning of step 520 and enquiry process models at the beginning of step 530. In the earlier stages, the team has identified entities that are implemented in other systems and that similar parts of the entity life history are handled. During Logical Design, attention can be given to identifying existing complete dialogues, update and enquiry processes that can be reused. Even if complete units can not be reused, there may be scope for reusing parts of logical access paths.
	At the end of stage 5, the complete Logical Design is returned to the Component Management Team for inclusion in the library.

Information Systems Engineering Library
Managing Reuse

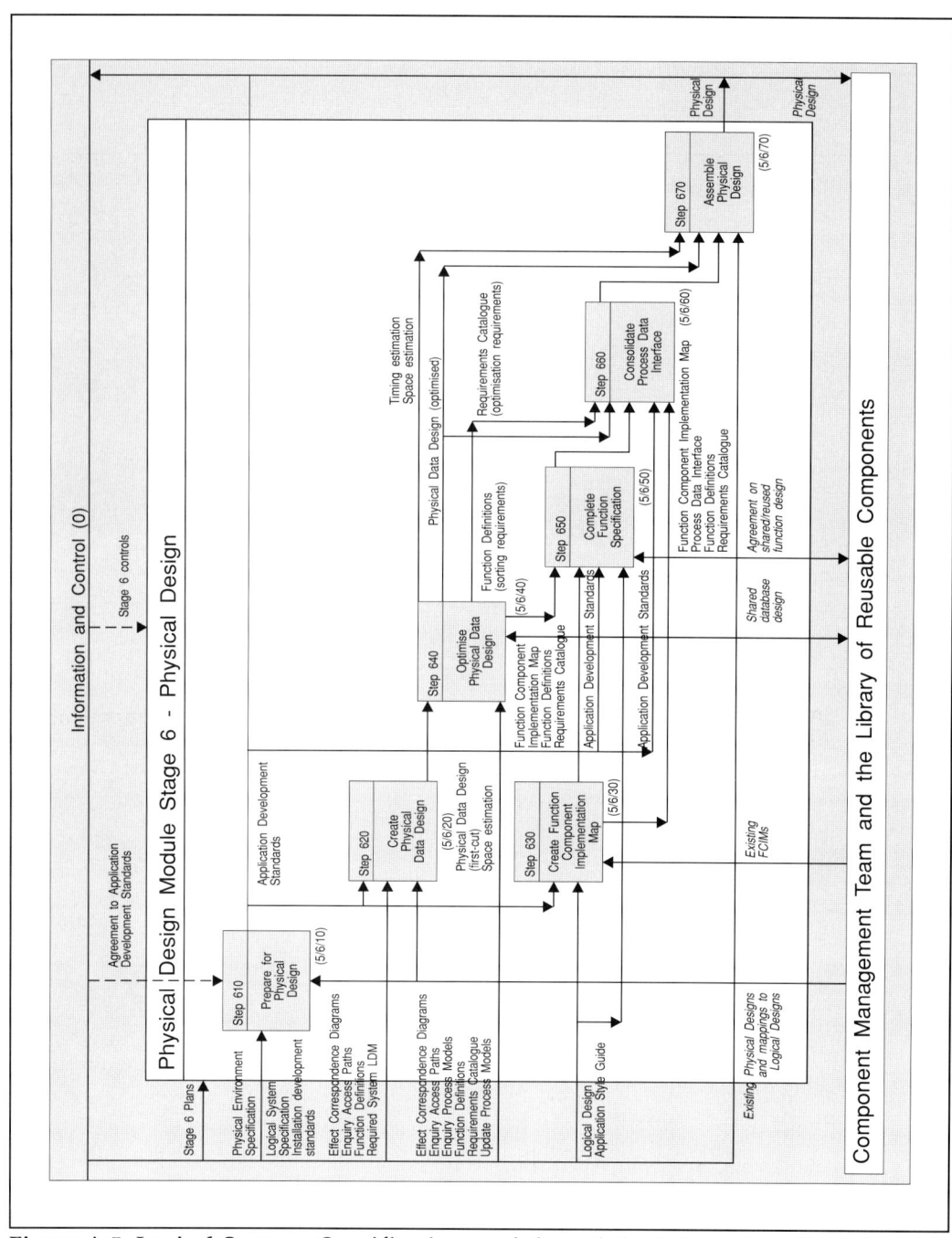

Figure A.5: Logical Systems Specification module and the information flows for reuse

Annex A
Tailoring SSADM for reuse

Physical Design module

> The need for management attention during Physical Design
>
> During Physical Design (see figure A.6), there is interaction between the project team and the database design function within the Component Management Team to ensure the reuse of existing data and reuse of existing database design where appropriate. A key goal at this stage is to reduce complexity of the application interfaces by interfacing applications through the database and avoiding transaction transfer files. In many large projects in which databases are not effectively shared, approximately six months of the project is spent building new functionality and three years building the interfaces. This time can be substantially reduced by reuse of a shared database.
>
> It is at this stage that the decisions to share must be implemented. Determined management attention is needed because of the tendency of projects to want *my database* or *my machine* without understanding the overheads they are imposing.

> Information flows
>
> The database design is developed by the Component Management Team in accordance with the project requirements and taking account of opportunities for reuse. The design is then recorded in the library.
>
> Where a project has identified reusable components at the Analysis or Logical Design stages, the existing Function Component Implementation Maps (FCIMs) will provide a link to the physical design components that are to be reused.
>
> Alternatively, the FCIMs of similar functions handling similar entities should be searched when a designer is seeking to identify reusable Physical Design components, knowing that the function being considered has not been previously implemented.
>
> Agreement is reached between the project and the Component Management Team concerning which function implementations are to be reused.

At the end of the stage, the Physical Design is returned to the Component Management Team for storage in the library.

Annex A
Tailoring SSADM for reuse

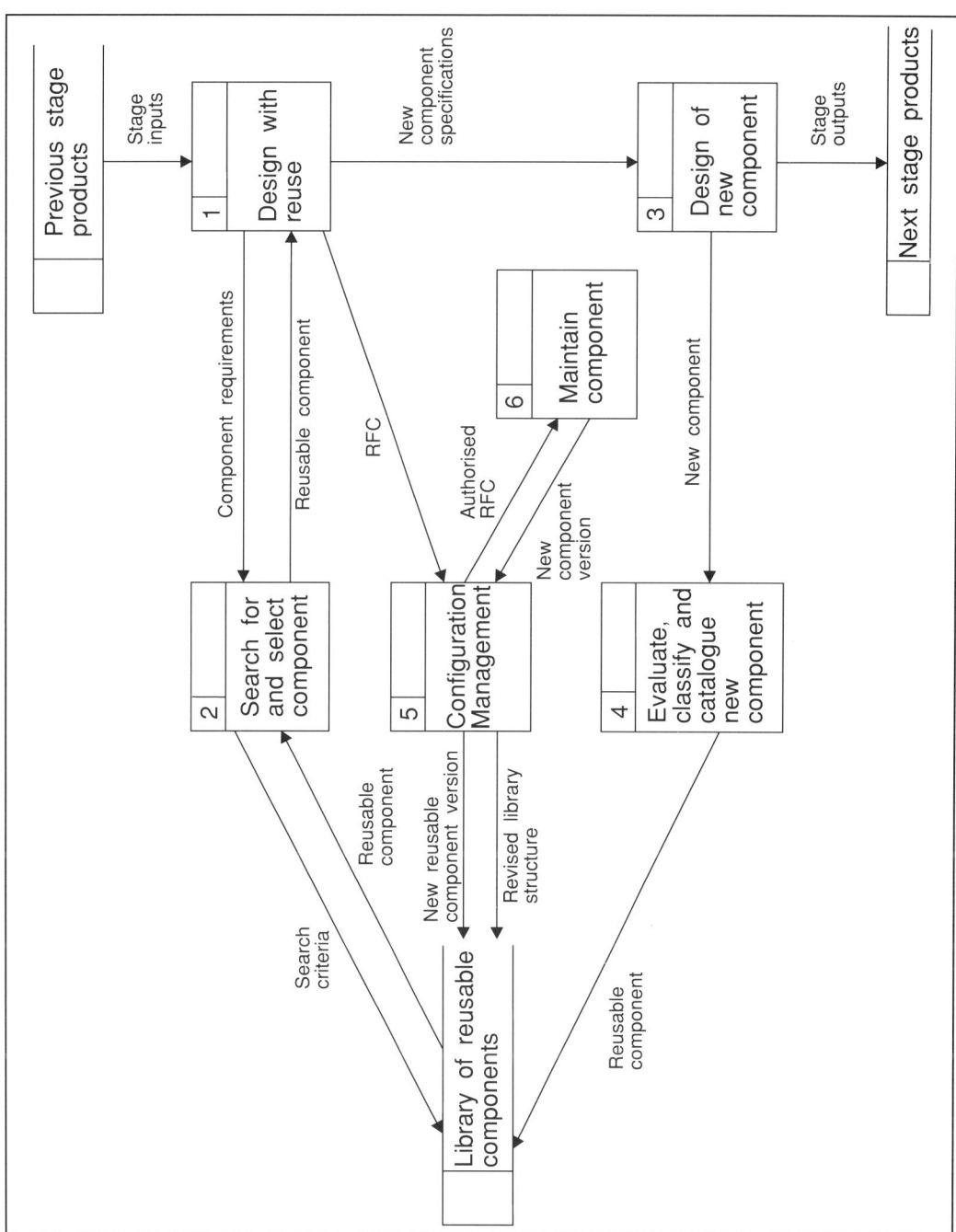

Figure A.6: Physical Design module and the information flows for reuse

Information Systems Engineering Library
Managing Reuse

B Bibliography

Information Systems   The Information Systems Engineering Library is
Engineering Library   published by CCTA and is available from HMSO
Publications Centre, PO Box 276, London SW8 5DT.

The following volumes are referenced in this publication:

Reverse Engineering
  ISBN: 0 11 330602 4

PCTE: An Overview
  ISBN: 0 11 330595 8

CASE: The Issues for Management
  ISBN: 0 11 330594 X

Appraisal and Evaluation   The Appraisal and Evaluation Library is published by
Library   CCTA and is available from HMSO Publications
Centre, PO Box 276, London SW8 5DT.

The following volume is referenced in this publication:

IT Infrastructure Support Tools
  ISBN: 0 11 330586 9

Information Management   The Information Management Library is published by
Library   CCTA and is available from HMSO Publications
Centre, PO Box 276, London SW8 5DT.

The following volume is referenced in this publication:

Corporate Data Modelling
  ISBN: 0 11 330614 8

Information Systems Guides   The Information Systems Guides, published by CCTA
and is available from John Wiley & Sons Ltd, Baffins
Lane, Chichester PO19 1UD.

The following volumes are referenced in this publication:

Information Systems Engineering Library
Managing Reuse

	IS Guide B Set: Systems Development Set ISBN: 0 471 92533 0
PRINCE documentation	The PRINCE Reference Manual is published by NCC Blackwell Ltd and is available from NCC Blackwell Ltd, 108 Cowley Road, Oxford, OX4 1JF ISBN 1 850 12012 6
SSADM documentation	The SSADM Version 4 Reference Manual is published by NCC Blackwell Ltd and is available from NCC Blackwell Ltd, 108 Cowley Road, Oxford, OX4 1JF ISBN 1 85554 004 5
Other publications	George Black, The Template Solution Software Management, November 1991 Department of Defence Trusted Computer System Evaluation Criteria, Office of Standards and Products, Maryland, 1985 DoD 5200.28-STD Prieto-Diaz, R., Domain Analysis: An Introduction, Software Engineering Notes, Vol. 15 no. 2, April 1990 pp- 47-54.

C Glossary

3-schema specification architecture
Looks at information systems in the context of the ANSI 3 schema architecture. It consists of a **conceptual** (qv), **external** (qv) and **internal schema** (qv).

access paths
The route to be taken through the Logical Data Model from an entry point to the entity, or entities, required for a particular piece of processing.

AD/Cycle
IBM's framework for information systems development tools.

ANSI
American National Standards Institute.

CASE
Computer Assisted Systems Engineering.

class hierarchy
A directed graph (qv) in which super-class (qv) nodes are divide into sub-class (qv) nodes.

CLUMP
Corporate Logical Units of Manageable Proportions.

COCOMO
COnstructive COst MOdel.

component management team
The executive arm of the Inter-Project Board with responsibility for the library of reusable components.

conceptual schema
Defines the scope of the IS system. Consists of the logical data model concerned with the provision of information support to business activities together with the inputs needed to keep the model up to date.

configuration management
The discipline of identifying components of a system to control changes to it and maintain its integrity throughout its life-cycle.

context diagrams
Illustrates the initial scope of the proposed system. It concentrates on the major inputs and outputs of the system and shows the external sources and recipients of system data.

copy reuse
The taking of a copy of a component for reuse. Sometimes known as cloning.

data model
Used to help define the scope of the system and ensure that the analysts have a clear understanding of the

	user's problems and requirements. The technique is used to build a model of the information flows and not to define the detail of the processing performed by the system.
directed graph	A diagrammatic representation of the concepts showing the relationship between them.
ECMA	European Computers Manufacturers' Association.
enquiry process model	A structure diagram for an enquiry processing requirement and the associated Operations List. The structure is based on the Enquiry Access Path.
enquiry access path	The route through the Logical Data Model from an entry point to the entity, or entities, required for a particular enquiry function.
entities	Anything in the real world, tangible or intangible, and groups or classes thereof about which information is held in the system.
ESCROW	A scheme where the source code or specification of a product is deposited with a third party for safe keeping.
external schema	Determines how users can access the information system. Is defined in functions and is implemented in dialogues within menus and/or the batch input/output system.
IED	DTI (Information Engineering Directorate).
inheritance	The sharing of attributes and operations among classes in a class hierarchy.
inter-project board	A board responsible for co-ordinating reuse between several projects.
internal schema	Maps the logical data model on to an implementation technology and provides access to the stored data.
IPR	Intellectual Property Rights.
IRDS	Information Dictionary resource System.

ISO	International Standards Organisation.
library	A store of components which can be reused between projects.
logical data model	Provides an accurate model of the information requirements of all or part of an organisation. This serves as a basis for file and database design, but is independent of any specific implementation technique or product.
LUMP	Logical Unit of Manageable proportions.
object class	A possibly infinite group of objects with similar properties, but with the same behaviour, relationships to other objects and the same semantics.
object instance	A single occurrence of an object class that has a unique identity, distinguishing it from other instances. Each instance has its own value for each attribute but shares the attribute names and operations with other instances of the class.
object-oriented	A method of organising software as a collection of discrete objects that incorporate both data structure and behaviour.
operation	A function or transformation that may be applied to or by objects in a class. All objects in the same class share the same operations.
PCTE	Portable Common Tools Environment.
PID	Project Initiation Document.
PRINCE	PRojects In Controlled Environments - CCTA's project management method.
process data interface	Documents how the Logical Data Model can be mapped onto the Physical Data design, showing how it interfaces with the Physical Processing Specification.
RECAST	Reverse engineering to CASE technology - a collaborative research project set up under the IED initiative. The project carried out research on reverse engineering of COBOL systems to SSADM.

	Contributors were; CCTA, LBMS and CSM, University of Durham. The RECAST method is to be published in the ISE Library.
relational data analysis	a method of deriving data structures which have the least redundant data and the most flexibility. It is the objective of this method to transform all relation to at least third normal form.
relationships	An association between two entities, or one entity and itself, to which all instances of the relationship must conform.
reusable component	A component of an information system which can be used by several systems.
RFC	Request for Change.
SCADA	Supervisory Control and Data Acquisition.
SSADM	Structured Systems Analysis and Design Method.
sub-class	A node in a data or processing class-hierarchy that represents a refinement of a super-class. A sub-class inherits the attributes of the super-class and adds its own specific attributes and operations. Also known as a sub-type.
super-class	A node in a data or processing class-hierarchy. A super-class records properties common to all its sub-classes. Also known as a super-type.
tailored reuse	The modification of a copy of an existing component.
three schema architecture	An architecture that provides three levels or views of a system. The conceptual level (the overall logical model), the external level (user or applications view of the system), and the internal level (the description of the physical implementation).
true reuse	Using an existing implemented component rather than a copy of it.

Index

benefits 7, 8, 11, 13, 18, 21, 22, 50, 55, 57, 63, 67, 71, 81, 89
component libraries 69
component library 38, 48, 59, 66, 67, 72, 74
component management team 11, 68, 72, 74, 76, 81, 82, 83, 84, 90, 91, 93-96, 98, 100, 101, 103, 105, 106, 111
configuration management 48, 51, 72, 74, 94, 111
copyright 2, 26
corporate data model 15, 93, 95, 98, 100
costs 7, 8, 11, 13, 19, 21-25, 60-62, 76, 77
external design 33, 35, 37, 38
feasibility study 60, 66, 76, 94, 96-98
formal methods 26, 46
Inland Revenue 17, 34, 42, 73, 86
inter-project board 11, 44, 59, 68, 69, 72, 73, 75-77, 81, 82, 83, 84, 93, 103, 111, 112
interoperability 54
legal issues 25, 26, 64
life-cycle 3, 7, 11, 15, 17, 18, 24, 39-41, 44, 47, 48, 59, 60, 66, 69, 71, 81, 90, 111
logical data model 14, 29-31, 40, 41, 74, 93, 95, 96, 111, 112, 113
maintenance 3, 8, 13, 20, 22, 25, 38-40, 60, 61, 63, 64, 76, 77, 79, 82, 84
National Health Service 16, 86
object-oriented 13, 14, 17, 21, 23, 24, 44, 46, 89, 113
 encapsulation 44
 inheritance 14, 44, 90, 112
OO 13, 26, 49
Ordnance Survey 16, 86
portability 23, 53, 80
PRINCE 3, 7, 72, 110, 113
programme board 59, 81
project board 11, 15, 44, 59, 60, 68, 69, 72, 73, 75-77, 81-84, 93, 96, 103, 111, 112
quality 3, 11, 13, 20, 25, 26, 40, 41, 46, 64, 66, 71, 72, 75, 76-79, 86, 87, 94
reengineering 26
repositories 25, 50-52, 74
repository 24, 48, 50, 51, 53
reverse engineering 24, 46-48, 62, 109, 113
risks 8, 11, 13, 21-23, 25, 26, 40, 53, 63, 78

SSADM 3, 7-9, 17, 27, 28, 35, 38-44, 47, 60, 61, 66, 76, 89, 90, 92, 94, 95, 98, 110, 113, 114
  data flow diagrams 90
  entity life histories 89, 90, 93, 95
  structural model 90
  sub-typing 89
support 3, 8, 21, 25, 27-31, 33, 34, 36-38, 42, 48, 51, 52, 62-65, 74, 77, 81, 83-87, 109, 111
three schema architecture 114
  conceptual schema 29, 31-34, 111
  external schema 31-33, 112
  internal schema 31, 34, 111, 112